The Search for Emma's Story

Dear Clem, Emmie Lou & Kevin

Happy reading as you
travel down memory lane
with Emma.

Love
Ophelia N. Weinheimer

The Search for Emma's Story

A Model for Humanities Detective Work

by Marian L. Martinello

with
Ophelia Nielsen Weinheimer

Photography by Thomas H. Robinson

TEXAS CHRISTIAN UNIVERSITY PRESS
FORT WORTH

Library of Congress Cataloging-in-Publication Data

Martinello, Marian L.
  The search for Emma's story.

  1. Beckmann, Emma, b. 1888.   2. German Americans—
Texas—Fredericksburg Region—Biography.
3. Fredericksburg Region (Tex.)—Biography.
4. Biography (as a literary form)—Case studies.
5. Ethnology—Texas—Case studies.   I. Weinheimer,
Ophelia Nielsen.   II. Title.
F394.F9B435   1987   976.4'65   [B]   86-30005
ISBN 0-87565-070-8

Design by Whitehead & Whitehead

This book is printed on acid-free material.

For my parents,
Helena Terenzio Martinello *and* Rocco Martinello
for teaching me to celebrate the lives
of all people

Contents

Illustrations	ix
Acknowledgements	xi
A Model for Humanities Detective Work	1
Orange Blossoms and Leg-o'-Mutton	11
The Wish List	45
Trial Marks	111
Cotton Bolls and Gingerbread	155
Finding Life Stories	201

Illustrations

Signpost Artifacts

Beckmann Wedding Portrait	10
Emma's Wish List	44
Watkins Bottle	113
Beckmann Victorian-style House	157

Items of Evidence

Location of Gillespie County, Texas	6
Map of Stonewall Area	7
Sauer-Beckmann Living History Farm	8
Beckmann Marriage License	14
U.S. Population Census of 1900	18, 19
Alma Scharnhorst Nielsen's Wedding Dress	21
Nielsen Wedding Portrait	23
Mayer Wedding Portrait	25
Behrens Wedding Portrait	27
Congregation of Trinity Lutheran Church, 1909	29
Lintel of Mayer Home	31
The Mayer Home	31
Beckmann Log House	36
Floor Plan of Log House	47
Sears Roebuck Catalog Items	49, 50, 51
The Mayer Children	55

Emma at Sixteen Years   57
Emma's School Class   59
Barnes' New National Reader   69
Emma's Baptismal Record   81
A Confirmation Class   86
Friendship Card   93
Valentine Card, ca. 1880   94
Alma Scharnhorst's Blouse   127
The Tatting Process   128, 129, 130
Map of Block in Fredericksburg—1902 and 1910   136, 137
Map of Block in Fredericksburg—ca. 1908   139
Wahrmund Millinery Store   141
Lungkwitz Millinery Store   143
Nimitz Hotel, 1891   143
Front and Back Porches of Victorian-style House   160, 161
Beckmann Henhouse   162
Beckmann Smokehouse   163
Beckmann Tank House   165
View of Outside Hallway from Within
    Victorian-style House   166
Floor Plan of Victorian-style House   167
Beckmann Victorian-style House: Children's Room   168
Beckmann Victorian-style House: Master Bedroom   169
Beckmann Parlor   171
Beckmann Kitchen   172, 173
Kitchen in Log House   175
Baptismal Records   177
Beckmann Barn   185
Interior of Beckmann Barn   185

Acknowledgements

ANY people contributed to my search for Emma's story and to the preparation of this book. While I assume sole responsibility for the authenticity and accuracy of the information and its interpretations, the work could not have been completed without the help of those who shared with me their skills, their knowledge, their artifacts, and their enthusiasm for humanities detective work. I express my deep and lasting appreciation to each and everyone who helped.

The search could not have gotten far without the assistance of Donald Schuch, Head Superintendent of the Lyndon B. Johnson State Historical Park at Stonewall, Texas, Kenneth Jenschke, Superintendent of Interpretation, and the staff members at the Sauer-Beckmann Living History Farmstead where Emma's Victorian-style house stands as it did in 1915–1918. In alphabetical order the staff members are: Denise Abendschein, Gary Bierschwale, Betty Klein, John Matthews, Ophelia Weinheimer, Bruce Thiele, and Ricky Weinheimer. I am also indebted to Bruce Smith of the Texas State Department of Parks and Wildlife for directing me to turn-of-the-century maps of Fredericksburg.

Members of the Albert-Stonewall-Fredericksburg community who provided me with artifacts and recollections of life in Emma's time are: Reverend Ernst Arhelger, Henry Beckmann, Margaret Bracher, Walter Behrens and his sisters Lydia and Cliftine, Christine Brautigaum Brodie, Tyrus Cox, Loreen Geistweidt, Ella Gold, Erna Oehler Hartmann, Edna Beckmann Hightower,

Paul Klein, Theo Lindig, Margareta and Hugo Manieus, Anna Meier, Hilda Moldenhauer, Ophelia Scharnhorst Neffendorf, Alma Scharnhorst Nielsen, Roger Ottmers, Ruth Mayer Ottmers, JoAnn Beckmann Schott, Vera and Marvin Schuch, Dorothy Uecker, Lina Bauer Uecker, and Charles Weinheimer.

C. E. Schmidt, local district manager for the Watkins Company, deserves recognition for his knowledge of the company's history and his willingness to share it with me.

Community agencies and institutions also made valuable information available. My appreciation is extended to Trinity Lutheran Church in Stonewall and to Bethany, Holy Ghost, and Zion Lutheran churches in Fredericksburg for allowing me access to their records. To all the people in the following organizations, I express my thanks: The Barker Center for Historical Research at the University of Texas at Austin; The Daughters of the Republic of Texas Library at the Alamo in San Antonio; the *Fredericksburg Standard;* the several county offices in the Gillespie County Courthouse, especially the Office of the County Clerk, the Office of the County Tax Assessor/Collector, and the Office of the County Judge; the Gillespie County Historical Society; the John Peace Library of The University of Texas at San Antonio; the Pioneer Memorial Library at Fredericksburg; the San Antonio Public Library; the Texas State Library in Austin; and the Institute of Texan Cultures at San Antonio.

Three very special people deserve a lion's share of the credit for all that is right and good about this book. They are my collaborator, Ophelia Nielsen Weinheimer; my photographer, Thomas H. Robinson; and Paul Weber, who typed the manuscript and also served as a first-class editor.

Ophelia Weinheimer was indeed my Dr. Watson. She kept me honest and on target throughout the two years of our collaboration on the project. She made it possible for me to meet people who had important information to share. She shared her knowledge of the community unstintingly with me. She buoyed my enthusiasm whenever it flagged. She dug up information that I thought was beyond finding and presented it to me with an enthusiasm that was infectious. In the process, she became my dear friend.

Acknowledgements

My photographer has an eye for detail and for the aesthetic. Thomas Harold Robinson gave much of himself to create illustrations for this book that, at times, seemed impossible to make. He sometimes joked about having to make pictures without light or film; on some occasions, he came close to doing just that. Even with primitive work conditions, Tom produced beautiful images that recreate the visual elements of Emma's story. His pictures have the clarity and perspective needed to develop viewers' abilities to see more than they might on their own.

Paul Weber's involvement with the project began with his preparation of the typed manuscript. He brought to that work his outstanding secretarial skills and a great deal more. Paul's own cultural background enabled him to read the manuscript with insight into Emma's lifestyle and with genuine interest in her story. As he did so, he served as an editor who asked probing questions and suggested important revisions. The book was improved by his touch.

It is with great pleasure that I acknowledge these many people who helped to make my inquiry into the everyday life of an ordinary person a learning experience that was also downright fun.

Marian L. Martinello
San Antonio, Texas

A Model for Humanities Detective Work

HIS is a detective story—a two-fold story. On the one hand, it recounts my inquiry into the life of an ordinary woman. On the other, it tells the findings that emerged from my search. It is a description and a model of humanities detective work that probes all sorts of artifacts—personal belongings, memorabilia, photographs and artworks, documents and personal papers, printed materials, toys, tools, work places, home furnishings and living quarters—for clues to the life of someone who lived in another place and time. The detective work is the inquiry, the creative questioning, the unexpected clues found in unsuspected places, and the hunches, deductions, inferences, and imaginings those findings spawn.

It is called *humanities* rather than historical detective work because its focus is on people and their experiences; it causes us to look from multidisciplinary perspectives to see them as whole persons who awaken, walk, talk, eat, work, want, need, achieve, think, feel, even dream. As humanities detectives, we ask questions, find clues, piece together the fabric of a life and revive that life in our imaginations. Humanities detective work uncovers the facts and calls upon imagination to fill in the gaps. It uses the processes of pointed questioning (who, what, where, when, how), hardnosed data gathering, and subjective inferring to find patterns in human lives. The result is that people and their experiences in times past come to life in our mind's eye. Then, and only then, does history become human.

This book is not intended for historians who wish to do the exhaustive research that establishes formal, academically impeccable history. But it does suggest first steps, especially for the novice inquirer into human experience: young students who, in this age of early technological specialization, risk losing touch with human experiences of the past. It is also for the amateur researcher and those who plan learning experiences for beginners: teachers, docents, scout leaders, museum educators—all who want to design historical projects that can capture and sustain the interest of the beginner in humanities research. Finally, it is for those who seek a model of inquiry for detecting the lives of historic personae in their own communities.

My central figure is Emma Beckmann. The chapters of this book, singly and collectively, reconstruct her story as they model an attic-trunk approach to reviving human experiences—an approach somewhat random in its selection of artifacts, concerned with immediately and locally available sources of information. I practiced an artist's inquiry: visual and imaginative yet also authentic because it dealt with Emma's total being at a specific time in her life.

The chapters of this book are organized according to the actual process of my inquiry. Emma's experiences are presented as I studied them; they became the topics of each chapter. I did not choose those topics; in a sense the artifacts did that for me. Each chapter begins by showing how one or two artifacts influenced my search. I call them signpost artifacts because they determined the direction of my investigation. While the data was being collected and especially after it was assembled, I could not help forming images of Emma living out the episodes of her life that my research documented, from her birth in 1888 to the time she moved into her Victorian-style house and reared her young children (ca. 1918). The scenarios played out in my imagination made her story come alive. And they did something more—they let me know the gaps in my knowledge, the missing links in Emma's story. Even so, imaginary scenarios must be recognized for what they are. Accordingly, each chapter has three separate but related sections:

Signpost Artifacts
Portfolio of Evidence (*artifacts, questions,*
    and interpretations)
Emma's Story (*imaginative scenarios,*
    fictionalized history)

Students and amateur researchers should find this organization helpful in focusing their thinking about their own historic personae. Teachers, group leaders, and museum educators will find it an effective model for creating *humanities puzzles* (organized collections of artifacts for student inquiry) that will engage today's young people with people of the past.

The signpost artifacts that guided my search were not always deliberately sought. Frequently, I stumbled upon them. For instance, newspaper ads, a standard guide to businesses in a town, were not the source of my information about shops in the turn-of-the-century town that Emma knew. I happened upon my guide while looking for information about cooking: a cookbook published by the local ladies' auxiliary in 1916 had twenty-five pages of advertisements by local businesses. There were other surprises, too. This book celebrates the elusive clues and chance findings that motivate and enliven humanities detecting.

The humanities detective must strike a delicate balance between narrowing the search and keeping it open to new directions. Openness permits all sorts of pathways to emerge; some are rich with new ideas. But so many potential directions can surface at one time that they suddenly become overwhelming. Too many at once can mask the purpose of the search. The novice, in particular, needs clear signposts at the onset of inquiry. A single, carefully selected artifact can give the inquiry a tangible place to start.

Each signpost artifact is a piece of evidence in the life story of its maker, owner, or user. Each can be intriguing in its own right because it may have some unique qualities and contain references to human experience that help the inquirer make connections between this and that, then and now. And each is also a piece of evidence that can prompt lots of questions—provocative ones, the type not dismissed lightly. The first part of every chapter presents these signposts for my inquiry and the questions they caused me to ask. My purpose is to engage the reader with the evidence, as I was engaged with it, and to offer a model of strategies for creative questioning—asking the type of questions that coax out the stories in things.

To be sure, my interpretations of the signpost artifacts yielded valuable information. Yet the significance of each signpost is probably best measured by the questions it caused me to ask, questions that led me to search for additional pieces of evidence which, in turn, generated more questions. Hence, each chapter contains a "Portfolio of Evidence," a section that I gathered to advance my inquiry. It contains reproductions of sources that I found in public and private libraries, attics, flea markets, churches and cemeteries, courthouses and private dwellings—wherever I could find a lead. Captions for each identify them and their sources. But as with the signpost artifacts, the questions that each inspires are the main content of this book. They are guides to contemplating the evidence, suggesting ways of wondering about and deciphering the meanings that material things hold about the life of an ordinary person. They are offered so that beginning researchers can try my line of inquiry and develop their own skills of humanities detective work.

The book goes from the process of searching to fact-finding, from contemplating to constructing, from seeing to knowing. Accompanying the visual representation of each piece of evidence in the portfolio sections and the questions I asked of it are descriptions of the clues I found, the interpretations I made, and the new questions that came to mind—questions I had not thought to ask before I had contemplated the object, document, or recollection. These are offered to match wits with the reader. Did I see everything there was to find? Did I interpret it in the way the reader does? What alternative interpretations might there be? What additional questions beg for answers? The reader is encouraged to contemplate, meditate, and challenge.

The last section of each chapter is titled Emma's Story. This section goes beyond the traditionally accepted limits of historical research to recreate the intangible and unverifiable human qualities of life experience. Here I record what I imagined about Emma from the evidence that I had collected. What did she do, say, see, feel, think, know, wonder, and dream about? There are no verifiable answers, just conjectures. But conjectures must be entertained before human stories can be found. Making an individual live again in the mind's eye can be more difficult than piecing together facts about one of that person's artifacts, whether an entire house or a pottery shard. Much inferring and hypothesizing is necessary to imagine a flesh and blood person going about daily doings from daybreak to nightfall—living again. But that is the ultimate goal of humanities detective work.

My Historic Persona

first came to know Emma Beckmann through her land— the place she called home for her entire life. Some see it as an inhospitable place. Emma lived in the Texas Hill Country where the thirsty juniper (or cedar, as the local people call the plant) competes for water with gnarled live oak and prickly pear cactus. Everything seems to exist on a thin layer of soil spread over massive limestone boulders. The land hardly seems fertile enough to farm.

Yet some speak reverently of this land by the Pedernales River. This is land that produced cotton and forage for cattle and sheep and deer. It still can. It boasts of its peaches, its produce, and its healthy stock.

Emma lived in the southeast quadrant of Gillespie County. The towns of Albert, Stonewall, and Luckenbach were important in her life. When Emma spoke of going to town, she most likely referred to a full day's trip to Fredericksburg, some sixteen miles from her home in Stonewall. Fredericksburg was then and still is the Gillespie County seat. It was founded by German immigrants in 1846, the year the Republic of Texas became one of the United States of America.

I came upon Emma's house when I first visited the Lyndon B. Johnson State Historical Park at Stonewall, where her homestead is preserved as a living history farm. The home and its neighboring buildings are maintained as they were from about 1915 to 1918 when Emma was a young mother. She knew the Johnson family through her children: Emma's daughter, Edna, often played with Lyndon Johnson's sister, Josefa. Edna recalls Josefa's visits to the Beckmann house and her own visits to the Johnson place just across the Pedernales River.

Emma's presence pervades her house. Stepping onto the farm, stepping into the log cabin, the kitchen, and the Victorian-style house is at first like entering a time capsule that was buried at the turn of the twentieth century. Drawn by Emma, I returned to the house several times. Each successive visit became for me a way to move back into time—to get in touch with Emma. On each visit I saw more. The questions began to flow.

My earliest questions sought facts about things: What style is the furniture? What patterns are on the quilts? What labels do we give these things in the kitchen, in the parlor, in the barn and

Gillespie County is in the heart of Texas. The county is darkened here to show its location.

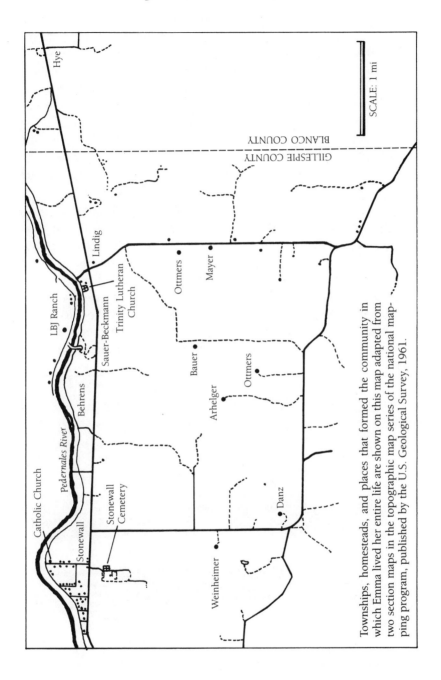

Townships, homesteads, and places that formed the community in which Emma lived her entire life are shown on this map adapted from two section maps in the topographic map series of the national mapping program, published by the U.S. Geological Survey, 1961.

sheds, on the table and under the beds? The questions seemed endless and, what is worse, the answers did not always help me better understand the history of the house or Emma, the person who gave the house something more than historical or architectural meaning. When I turned my attention back to Emma, the woman who made the house a home, I realized why I had an earlier sense of intrigue with the place. Detecting the human being behind an artifact is often far more exciting than identifying the object in isolation from its human referents. Studying a house to uncover information about people who lived in it is more like solving a mystery than studying the house for itself alone.

When I started to research Emma's story, I found that books and articles provided only bits and pieces of information relevant to my line of inquiry. Early in my search, I had no choice but to consult primary sources: photographs, county records, local newspapers, magazines and catalogs of the period, church records, census reports and, of course, objects themselves—the things of Emma's material culture. I had to learn how to "read" them. I also had to learn how to consult the people of the Hill Country, especially the women of Emma's generation who could

The Sauer-Beckmann Living History Farmstead on the Lyndon B. Johnson State Historical Park at Stonewall, Texas. The Sauer family owned and farmed this land before the Beckmanns, hence the hyphenated name for this historic site.

remember what it was like to live in their communities around the turn of the century and maybe even recall Emma herself. In private homes, nursing homes, and local businesses, I found people who could answer my questions about the place that Emma knew. These were conversations, not formal oral histories, and they gave me information not available elsewhere.

In searching for Emma's story I learned some history. Generally, I learned about rural central Texas in the early twentieth century. More specifically, I learned about the lives of girls and women of that time growing up on the farm in a German-Texan community. Particularly, I learned about the everyday and special-day life of an ordinary person who was called Emma and about the lives of others of her time and place.

Emma's story is not in history books. Neither are those of other historic personae whose lives readers of this book may choose to study. Clues to their stories are in the memories of old-timers and in the antiques of their culture. Although death and deterioration remove evidence, humanities detective work can uncover the pieces and reassemble them to discover the patterns of lives already lived. A special magic pervades the process of inquiring into human experiences of the past. It is felt in the thrill of the search, the excitement of the find, and especially in the empathy the humanities detective may develop toward others of there and then, of here and now, indeed of someone in someplace in anytime.

Signpost Artifact One: Wedding portrait of Emma Mayer and Emil Beckmann.

two

Orange Blossoms and Leg-o'-Mutton

MMA and Emil Beckmann look out from their wedding portrait in the hallway that connects the front and back porches of their house. I saw many things that had been theirs when I first visited the Beckmann house, but it was the wedding portrait that I kept returning to. Nothing else captured my interest as quickly or held it as long as that picture. It told me what Emma and Emil looked like, but it also prompted lots of questions.

I wondered about Emma as a person. To my knowledge, she had accomplished nothing extraordinary. That, in itself, made her special. I wanted to know about her, to understand her, and to find out how she was connected to her place and her time.

The wedding portrait, rich with hints about the young couple and their wedding, fascinated me. The more I looked at it, the more I saw: Emma's dark hair and eyes, her intense expression, the bleached-out whiteness of her dress, the tiny waist, the visible tip of her shoe, the shadows beneath her dress, her headdress and buttoned gloves, so bright against Emil's darker hand. What, I wondered, would Emma say to me if I could move back in time. At that moment, I decided to search for Emma.

The framed picture hanging from the molding of the Beckmann hallway was difficult to study. And I couldn't be sure that it was an original. One day early in my search for Emma's story, I was poking around Fredericksburg, the town closest to Stonewall, for ideas and artifacts. I stopped to look at old photographs in one of the local antique shops. The woman behind the counter pleasantly commented, "Wouldn't it be something to find someone you knew." And behold! As she said that, I turned over a photo to find Emma and Emil looking out at me from their wedding portrait. For one dollar, I purchased an original copy of that picture to take home and study many times over.

As I studied the photograph, my first thoughts were of Emma's appearance. Through a magnifying glass, I noted her rounded face, shortened in appearance by some curly wisps of a pompadour that dips down over her forehead. Emma's dark hair is pulled back from her face and seems secured at the nape of her neck. I guess that her tresses were long. Her dark eyes seem to be looking directly at me. (Had she been instructed to look directly into the camera?) The gaze is intense; the eyes have the largeness of youth. Emma has the look of a little girl here. *How old was she when she married?*

Emil seems fairer of hair and eyes, too, by comparison with his bride. His eyes are set closer together than Emma's, and his mouth is fuller. He looks older, perhaps by a few years, but still of Emma's generation. *Was he?*

Emil's hands are darker than his face and appear roughened. Veins stand out. His work was, no doubt, physical and out-of-doors. Yet his fingernails are almost as light as Emma's gloves.

The groom's highly polished shoes show dust in their creases. His suit does not fit him as well as Emma's dress fits her—the pants drape over his instep and heel; the crease is off-center.

Emma's dress has a high lace-edged collar and leg-o'-mutton sleeves. Just beneath the blouson bodice, Emma's waist is narrow and well-defined. She must have been wearing a corset. *Was she wearing her mother's wedding dress?*

A painted backdrop is behind the couple. I reasoned that the photograph was made by a photographer because only they owned backdrops of this type. But I could find no photographer's name or location on the photo; none is embossed on the poster board on which the picture is mounted. At first I thought that the picture was made in a studio. But some pieces of evidence within the picture itself contradict that assumption: the toe of Emil's shoe has cast a shadow directly beneath it. Emma's dress is so bleached by light that details are imperceptible. And little tufts of something appear at the backdrop's base. Some viewers think it's grass. I think that it's the fringed edge of a carpet. Maybe the backdrop was hung from a porch framework and the picture taken out-of-doors. Or perhaps the couple is standing on a rug in a studio. *Who was the photographer? Where was the portrait made? When was it made—on the Beckmanns' wedding day or at some other time? What about a celebration—did they have one? Was their wedding like any I knew? What happened on that day?*

Countless questions begged for answers. The evidence I collected in search of those answers is contained in this chapter's "Portfolio of Evidence." Each piece holds a clue—sometimes several clues—to Emma and Emil Beckmann's wedding day and the person who was Emma, the subject of this search, the central character of this real-life story.

The "Emma's Story . . ." section of this chapter offers an imaginative description of Emma's wedding day, reconstructed from the clues of my collected evidence.

Portfolio of Evidence

HE marriage license and certificate for Emma and Emil Beckmann was found in the Gillespie County records of marriages. These records are housed in the County Clerk's Office in the courthouse that stands on the public square in Fredericksburg. The record shows Emma's maiden name to be Mayer. The license was issued on December 9, 1907, by Herman Usener, then county clerk. The couple was united in marriage the next day, December 10, 1907, by M. Heinrich, who held the title of Pastor of Albert, Texas.

Someone, perhaps Pastor Heinrich, apparently made a trip to Fredericksburg on December 19 of that year and carried the Beckmann marriage certificate to the Gillespie County Clerk's office for filing. Sixteen miles was no small distance to travel by horse and buggy, so perhaps Pastor Heinrich waited to make the trip until he had several records to file or other business in town. It took Herman Usener three months to record the marriage; it was entered on March 1, 1908. (Paperwork at the courthouse

THE STATE OF TEXAS }
County of Gillespie }

No. *2933*

To any Judge of the County or District Court, Regularly Licensed or Ordained Minister of the Gospel, Jewish Rabbi, or Justice of the Peace in and for said County of Gillespie, Greeting:

You are Hereby Authorized to Solemnize the Rites of Matrimony

Between Mr. *Emil Beckmann* and Miss *Emma Mayer*

and make due return to the Clerk of the County Court of said County within sixty days thereafter, certifying your action under this License.

WITNESS my official signature and seal of office, at office in Fredericksburg the *9* day of *December* A. D. 190*7*.

Herman Usener
Clerk of County Court, Gillespie County.

By_____Deputy.

I, *M Heinrich*, hereby certify that on the *10* day of *December* A. D. 190*7*. I united in Marriage *Mr Emil Beckmann* and *Miss Emma Mayer*. the parties above named.

WITNESS my hand this *10* day of *December* A. D. 190*7*.

M. Heinrich. Pastor
Albert. Texas

Returned and filed for record the *19* day of *December* 190*7*., and recorded the *2* day of *March* 190*8*.

*Herman Usener*_____County Clerk.
*A W Petmecky*_____Deputy.

Marriage license and certificate for Emma and Emil Beckmann.

must have been heavy or the pace of work slower than it is today, or perhaps the county clerk had a variety of jobs to do.)

The name *M. Heinrich* appears on the marriage certificate as Pastor of Albert. The town of Albert is adjacent to Stonewall, and today there are Catholic, Christadelphian, and Lutheran churches in the community. *What was Pastor Heinrich's religious denomination?*

Ophelia Nielsen Weinheimer, a life-long resident of Emma's community and a member of Trinity Lutheran Church, knew that M. Heinrich had been the pastor of that congregation at the time Emma and Emil were married.

Several members of the Stonewall community suggested that I talk with a former member of the Trinity congregation, Rev. Ernst Arhelger (b. 1899 in Albert), who retired in Fredericksburg. In response to my questions, Reverend Arhelger told me:

> Rev. Max Heinrich was pastor of Trinity Lutheran from 1904–1913. During his pastorate, there was a church, the second for the congregation, built in 1904 to accommodate an increasing congregation.
>
> On two Sundays of every month, the pastor would conduct services at other communities and Trinity

would have no service. Pastor Heinrich actually served three local communities. When there were no services at the church on those Sundays the pastor was in other communities, the people of Albert-Stonewall would visit each other in their homes. Weddings, too, were usually at home rather than in church.

Reverend Arhelger volunteered additional information which raised new questions:

> Until 1950, services were held in the German language. Trinity at Albert-Stonewall was the last congregation in the Southern District of the American Lutheran Church to have all services in German.

Did Emma and Emil exchange their vows in German?
According to Reverend Arhelger, German would have been the language of Emma and Emil's wedding ceremony. I asked the present pastor of Trinity Lutheran for permission to examine church ledgers for 1907. He made early church records available to me. Their brown-edged pages with German titles listed name after name of church members in finely penned script. In some cases, one person's life could be traced from baptism to burial with other significant religious ceremonies along the way. The reference to Emma and Emil's marriage was entered in pen and ink like the other entries. The human quality of handwritten records caused images of Emil and Emma and Pastor Heinrich to form in my mind's eye.

The entry numbered sixteen on the *Trau* (German, "marriage") register for 1907 confirms the date of the wedding as the tenth of December and Reverend Arhelger's statement that German was the official language of the church at that time.

The document also revealed that Emil was a resident of Stonewall and twenty-five years old when he married. Only nineteen, Emma was six years younger than her groom. Her home was in Albert. Then I noticed that three *Zeugen* (German, "witnesses") carried the Beckmann name and one had Emma's maiden name.

My hunch was that Olga Beckmann was Emil's sister and that Max and Otto were his brothers; similarly, Ella Mayer could have been Emma's sister. Sometimes familial relationships can confuse the outsider; so many people are named that it becomes difficult to grasp their relationships. In this case, the descendants confirmed my guess.

In the local public library I found microfilm copies of the U.S. Population Census of 1900 for Gillespie County. I had to scan all handwritten entries for the county, because district borders have changed since 1900, until I came to the entries transcribed and presented on pages 18 and 19. This valuable find, a rich store of information about these families, confirmed my hunches about the relationship of the witnesses to the principals of the wedding. Further, I discovered that Emma's parents were named Ferdinand and Augusta and that Mr. Mayer, Emma's father, had been born in Texas. That meant that Emma's paternal grandparents had probably been among the early immigrants from Germany. Besides her younger sister, Ella, Emma had two younger brothers. Emma was a firstborn to parents who farmed, owned their own land free of mortgage, were literate, and could speak English. I surmised that Emma may have enjoyed special status in a family of comfortable means. This document also gave me Emma's birthday: February 1, 1888. And from it I knew that Emma had attended school as a child.

Both of Emil's parents were born in Germany. Otto and Max were Emil's brothers and Olga his sister. All members of the family were literate and could speak English. Emil was listed as a farm laborer in 1900, so he must have been working on his father's farm at that time. The Beckmann family owned its own farmland like the Mayers. But Emil's parents were older than Emma's and he had many more siblings (ten children are listed in the census; local residents of Stonewall put the total number of Beckmann children at twelve and the total number of Mayer children at four). Emil was not a firstborn, either. I felt that Emma had known a lifestyle in growing up that was different from the one her husband had experienced. I couldn't prove it, but it became a compelling hypothesis—one that lurked behind many questions and directions of my continuing search.

My preconceived notions about weddings taking place on weekends caused me to feel certain that *Das Wochenblatt,* a Fredericksburg local newspaper, would have a December 9 or 10 issue, a weekend issue. Unfortunately, the issues for the year 1907 were lost in the microfilm copies at the Fredericksburg Public Library and the offices of the *Fredericksburg Standard,* the successor to *Das Wochenblatt.* Still curious about the day of the week Emma had for her wedding day, I consulted a perpetual calendar. To my surprise, the tenth of December 1907 fell on Tuesday! *Why would a young woman choose so lackluster a weekday as Tuesday for her wedding?* A December wedding was not unusual among farmers, who have less pressing chores in late fall. But the Tuesday wedding intrigued me. Some have told me that Tuesday is reserved for celebrations and special services in the Evangelical Lutheran church. Others suggest that it might have been the day when the itinerant minister was in the area. No one seems to know for sure.

What about the weather on that date?

Finding out what the weather was like on the tenth of December 1907 was more difficult than I thought. Newspapers did not carry weather reports at that time. What I found is from the *Monthly Weather Review and Annual Summary* of the U.S. Department of Agriculture Weather Bureau. Of the reporting stations near Stonewall and Albert, Fredericksburg is the closest. If we assume that Stonewall-Albert had the same weather conditions as Fredericksburg for the month of December, it is likely that Emma and Emil had a nice day for their wedding. The mean temperature for the month was almost 60 degrees F, with a low of 28 and a high of 74 and next to no rainfall. December 10, 1907, was probably sunny and warm at least during the afternoon hours.

Now questions about the wedding itself reemerged. *What could I find out about Emma's wedding garments? At what time of day did the wedding take place? Where did it occur? What kind of celebration did they have? When was the wedding portrait made? By whom?*

I spoke to Alma Scharnhorst Nielsen (b. 1891 near Blanco, Texas, mother of Ophelia Weinheimer) about her wedding in 1912. She told me:

> The minister came to the house for an afternoon wedding at about three o'clock. The Nielsen band entertained menfolk outside at my wedding. Dinner was served in the house; people took turns eating. We had pork and trimmings, rice—sweet rice—and sweet potatoes from the smokehouse made into potato salad.

Township or other division of county: Justice Precinct No. Three (3)—Enumerated by me on the 23rd and 25th days of June,

LOCATIONS		NAME			RELATION	PERSONAL DESCRIPTION								
Number of dwelling-house in the order of visitation	Number of family in the order of visitation	Name of each person whose place of abode on June 1, 1900 was in this family.	Enter surname first, then the given name and middle initial, if any.	Include every person living on June 1, 1900. Omit children born since June 1, 1900.	Relationship of each person to the head of the family.	Color or race	Sex	Date of Birth	Year	Age at last birthday	Whether single, married, widowed, or divorced	Number of years married	Mother of how many children	Number of these children living
1	2	3			4	5	6	7		8	9	10	11	12
181	183	Mayer, Ferdinand			Head	W	M	July	1859	40	M	13		
		Mayer, Augusta			Wife	W	F	August	1865	34	M	13	4	4
		Mayer, Emma			Daughter	W	F	Feb	1888	12	S			
		Mayer, Ella			Daughter	W	F	April	1890	10	S			
		Mayer, Edgar			Son	W	M	October	1892	7	S			
		Mayer, Hugo			Son	W	M	June	1896	3	S			

Enumerated on the 19th and 20th days of June, 1900, Henry F. Kirchhoff, Enumerator

		Beckmann, Hermann			Head	W	M	April	1843	57	M	27		
		Beckmann, Mary			Wife	W	F	Jan	1853	47	M	27	12	12
		Beckmann, Otto			Son	W	M	Feb	1878	22	S			
		Beckmann, Hanna			Daughter	W	F	April	1879	21	S			
		Beckmann, Emil			Son	W	M	Dec	1881	18	S			
		Beckmann, August			Son	W	M	October	1883	16	S			
		Beckmann, Olga			Daughter	W	M	Jan	1885	15	S			
		Beckmann, Emily			Daughter	W	F	March	1887	13	S			
		Beckmann, Ottilie			Daughter	W	F	August	1889	10	S			
		Beckmann, Max			Son	W	M	June	1891	8	S			
		Beckmann, William			Son	W	M	Jan	1893	7	S			
		Beckmann, Heulda			Daughter	W	F	Jan	1896	4	S			

This transcription of excerpts from the U.S. Population Census of 1900 contains entries for the

1900, Henry F. Kirchhoff . . . Enumerator

	NATIVITY		CITIZENSHIP			OCCUPATION, TRADE, OR PROFESSION of each person TEN YEARS of age and over		EDUCATION			
lace of birth of each person and parents of ach person enumerated. If born in the Jnited States, give the State or Territory; if f foreign birth, give the Country only.											
Place of birth of this PERSON	Place of birth of FATHER of this person	Place of birth of MOTHER of this person	Year of imigration to the United States	Number of years in the United States	Naturalization	Occupation	Months not employed	Attended school (in months)	Can read	Can write	Can speak English
13	14	15	16	17	18	19	20	21	22	23	24
·xas	Germany	Germany				Farmer	0		Yes	Yes	Yes
ermany	Germany	Germany							Yes	Yes	Yes
·xas	Texas	Germany				At school		10	Yes	Yes	Yes
·xas	Texas	Germany				At school		10	Yes	Yes	Yes
·xas	Texas	Germany									
·xas	Texas	Germany									
·ermany	Germany	Germany	1852	47		Farmer	0		Yes	Yes	Yes
·ermany	Germany	Germany	1852	48							
·xas	Germany	Germany				Farm laborer	0		Yes	Yes	Yes
·xas	Germany	Germany							Yes	Yes	Yes
·xas	Germany	Germany				Farm laborer	0		Yes	Yes	Yes
·xas	Germany	Germany				Farm laborer	9	9	Yes	Yes	Yes
·xas	Germany	Germany				At school		9	Yes	Yes	Yes
·xas	Germany	Germany				At school		9	Yes	Yes	Yes
·xas	Germany	Germany				At school		9	Yes	Yes	Yes
·xas	Germany	Germany				At school		7½			
·xas	Germany	Germany									
·exas	Germany	Germany									

.milies of Ferdinand Mayer and Hermann Beckmann.

We had no wedding cake but there were lots of layer cakes and cookies for the guests to enjoy with strong coffee.

The price of my wedding dress and other things was twenty-five dollars. I made my dress from white batiste. I didn't have flowers—I was married in the wintertime. But I had a wax orange blossom headdress that I ordered from the Montgomery Ward catalog. That's where I got my husband's boutonniere too.

We didn't exchange rings during the marriage ceremony. My husband gave me the ring that would be my wedding ring when we became engaged. The wedding portrait was usually made after the wedding. It could be weeks or months later. We rode to the photographer in a one-horse buggy, carrying our wedding clothes. The photographer usually had an artificial bouquet if you wanted one. Heyland was the photographer in Fredericksburg. He made one dozen prints of the picture. But we had ours made by another photographer in Blanco. We didn't like the pictures Heyland made.

Reverend Arhelger confirmed that weddings were afternoon events. He added:

Usually there were no songs—no music. The bride and groom would sit on chairs set out for them so that friends and relatives could visit with them.

So, it seems that Emma would have been married in her parents' home in the afternoon of December 10. Now I wondered about what that house was like. It was probably filled with guests. Just the two immediate families would have counted almost twenty people. Surely friends and neighbors attended too; many of them would have stayed to eat a late-afternoon dinner with the bride and groom. The meal was probably much like the one Mrs. Nielsen described for her wedding. Perhaps the Beckmanns had music, perhaps not. It probably depended on whether there were any musical members of either family.

Mrs. Nielsen's evidence about her wedding clothes brought me back to my earlier line of inquiry into Emma's clothing.

Alma Scharnhorst made this dress for her marriage to Sofus Nielsen in 1912. Made in two pieces, the batiste blouse and skirt were worn over a corset, camisole, and petticoat. *Photographed by permission of Mrs. Alma Scharnhorst Nielsen, Fredericksburg, Texas.*

Emma must have worn a corset. Not only does her cinched waist in her wedding portrait suggest that, but so did Mrs. Nielsen's wedding clothes. When I placed Mrs. Nielsen's gown on a contemporary dress form for a woman of slender build, the ends of the skirt's waistband would not meet. The separation was several inches in length. Pins had to be used to hold the skirt on the dress form.

Examining the tucks, the lace inserts, and the drawn thread-work on the bodice and skirt made me keenly aware of Mrs. Nielsen's skill as a seamstress. Sewing skill must have been of paramount importance among women of the Texas Hill Country. And since not all the stitching was done by hand, I guessed that the sewing machine figured prominently in a young woman's set of household tools as well as in her education for the role of wife and homemaker. Mrs. Nielsen took pride in the beauty of the wedding dress she made. My hunch is that Emma made her own dress too and that she felt a similar pride of workmanship.

The fabric of white batiste is light for late fall, but it is very workable: its handkerchief-like softness bends to the dressmaker's will and drapes on the body or, when starched, stands away to the degree desired. To prepare the dress for the photograph, Mrs. Nielsen's daughter, Ophelia Weinheimer, ironed it with an extra touch of starch to give the fabric body. Since batiste was a popular fabric for rural brides in Texas in the early nineteen-hundreds, Emma probably made her dress of that white fabric. I felt quite sure that Emma did not wear her mother's wedding dress, but I needed proof.

Mr. and Mrs. Mayer's wedding portrait from the year 1887, given to me by Emma's nephew, Hugo Manieus, presented clear-cut evidence that Emma was not wearing her mother's dress in her wedding portrait. Mrs. Mayer's dress was not white and was of a style significantly different from Emma's. At twenty-three, Mrs. Mayer appears to have been stockier than her daughter was at nineteen. Nonetheless, the corset shaped them both.

There seems to have been less change in men's clothing from 1887 to 1907 in the Texas Hill Country. Mr. Mayer's suit is not very different from Emil's or, for that matter, the suit Sofus Nielsen wore in 1912.

The pose taken by the Mayers in 1887 demonstrates an in-

This wedding portrait of Alma Scharnhorst and Sofus Nielsen shows the bride wearing the dress pictured on page 21. *Reproduced by permission of Mrs. Alma Scharnhorst Nielsen, Fredericksburg, Texas.*

teresting difference from that of Emma and Emil in 1908 or Alma and Sofus Nielsen in 1912. Ferdinand Mayer is seated while his bride stands. But Emma and Emil, like Alma and Sofus, stand together in their wedding portrait. *Was the relationship of husband and wife becoming more egalitarian after the turn of the century? Or was it merely that photographic styles were different?* Mrs. Nielsen remembers the photographer who took her wedding portrait telling her and Mr. Nielsen to "stand there."

The question of who took the photograph of Emma and Emil in their wedding attire continued to intrigue me, especially after Mrs. Nielsen had told me that brides of her day used Heyland, the photographer in Fredericksburg. It seemed plausible that Heyland had been the photographer for Emma and Emil's wedding portrait too. Yet, I couldn't help but wonder why Heyland had not put his name on their photograph; I had come across many photos made at Heyland's studio, and all bore clear labels. Besides, Mrs. Nielsen was talking about her experiences with weddings and wedding portraiture in 1912. *Had things been different in 1907?*

To check on whether Heyland had been in business in 1907, I looked for but could not find a city directory for that year or, for that matter, any others of the period. The local newspaper, *Das Wochenblatt,* for the time in question did not carry photographers' ads (in fact, the paper carried relatively few ads by today's standards). So I began to search for other photographs bearing a photographer's identification and taken in the years between 1905 and 1910.

As a young wife, Emma lived on a relatively secluded farm. According to Walter Behrens, his mother, Maria Nielsen Behrens, was Emma's closest neighbor and a good friend. Maria Nielsen and Edmund Behrens were married on September 11, 1908, some nine months after Emma and Emil took their vows. They lived in a frame house on land adjoining the Beckmann farm.

Maria and Edmund Behrens stand in front of a backdrop on a wooden floor. Mr. Behrens is resting his hand on a small table. They stand together just as Emma and Emil did in their portrait. The photograph appears to have been made in a studio, and the mark is Heyland's. This told me that Heyland was in business in 1908. He could have been in business just nine months earlier

Wedding portrait of Ferdinand and Augusta Mayer, married in 1887. Mrs. Mayer was twenty-three at the time and Mr. Mayer, twenty-eight. *Photograph reproduced courtesy of Mr. and Mrs. Hugo Manieus, Albert, Texas.*

when Emma and Emil were married. Therefore, it was possible that he had made the Beckmann portrait too, but some pieces of evidence argued against that: Emma and Emil's wedding portrait may have been taken out-of-doors rather than in a studio, and it bore no photographer's imprint. All the pictures I had seen which were attributed to Heyland had been taken indoors and bore his name.

Reverend Arhelger remembered a photographer who lived just across the Pedernales River in the Stonewall area. His name was Benner. Of the dozens of photographs I perused in the living rooms and attics of local families and those I found in the antique stores and flea markets of Stonewall and Fredericksburg, I could find none that bore Benner's name. Then one surfaced. Mrs. Nielsen had it in her collection: a photograph of the congregation of Trinity Lutheran Church in front of the church building, marked with the date January 1, 1909, and Benner's name.

If Benner was a local photographer, it would have been simpler and maybe less expensive for Emma and Emil to have their portrait made by him than at Heyland's Fredericksburg studio. But I had to admit that there were gaps in the verifiable information I had found. I did not have proof that Benner was taking pictures in 1907. Nor could I be certain that Heyland's name always appeared on his photographs. Then there was the possibility that another itinerant photographer might have been passing through the Albert-Stonewall area in December 1907. This mystery remains unsolved. I may never know who took the Beckmann wedding portrait.

I consulted Reverend Arhelger again about Trinity Lutheran Church and congregation, asking him to tell me all he could about the church as a social institution.

> The first church building stood at the place where the present parsonage is located. The congregation worshipped in this building until the second building was erected in 1904. At that time, the first church building was converted into a parsonage. Until this time, the pastor lived in Stonewall. This second church building stood about where the present building is located, facing east. In this building, the Trinity congregation wor-

The wedding portrait of Mr. and Mrs. Edmund Behrens, who were married on September 11, 1908, bears the name of the photographer and his location. Note the backdrop, the floor, and the table. Note also the direction and the intensity of the light on the subjects and their pose. *Photograph reproduced courtesy of the Behrens' children, San Antonio, Texas.*

shiped until in 1928 the third and present building was built.

Church services started at 10:30 or 11:00 A.M. People brought their lunches. There were tables under the live oak trees where families would eat and visit.

At 2:00 P.M. Sunday school was held. Some parents attended the school; some visited with one another while the children were being instructed. After Sunday school, some families would stop at the home of grandparents or others to visit with them before they went home.

The church was an important social institution for the community. The Lindig pasture was used as a picnic area. Once a year, a picnic was held there in the summer for the whole community. They would have a barbecue of roasted meat. They would have a service in the morning and a program of entertainment in the afternoon.

It seems, then, that Emma's social life may have been largely defined by the group activities associated with the church.

Based on what Reverend Arhelger remembered, the house that appears behind the church and to the left in the photograph was probably the one in which services were held until the church was built, when it became the parsonage. Interestingly, its architectural style is similar to that of the Victorian house in which I first "met" Emma.

A romantic image crossed my mind's eye: Emma walking down the aisle of the church dressed in her wedding finery. I immediately recognized an erroneous assumption—my own experience with weddings was not Emma's. I had enough evidence to support the idea that Emma and Emil were typical of their community in their time. Emma's wedding dress was styled in exactly the fashion of Texas Hill Country women who became brides during the first decades of the twentieth century. Whether or not this was high fashion, their wedding gowns were of a style they all knew and accepted: the high neck, long leg-o'-mutton sleeves, front blouson-puffed bodice, and cinched waist. They probably all made their own dresses out of white batiste, decorating sleeves, long skirt, and neckline with tucks and lace inserts. Also typical of

The congregation of Trinity Lutheran Church was photographed in front of the church on January 1, 1909. The pastor is standing in the center of the front line of parishioners; he holds a book in his left hand. This was probably Reverend Heinrich, the pastor who married Emma and Emil. Children and young people comprise the front row. Apparently neither Emil nor Emma is pictured. Emma would have been actively involved in the church at that time, but Emil probably was not. *Photograph reproduced courtesy of Mrs. Alma Scharnhorst Nielsen, Fredericksburg, Texas.*

weddings in their community was the home ceremony and simple celebration. Emma never took a bride's walk down the aisle of Trinity Lutheran Church. She and Emil must have been married at her parents' home. *Where was that house? What did it look like?*

If you travel south from Trinity Lutheran Church, along the road to Albert, you come upon an old Victorian-style stone house identified by community members as the house of Ferdinand and Augusta Mayer, Emma's parents. The lintel above the front door bears the name of F. Mayer and the date of 1899. *Did this house look the same when Emma was living there?* My answer to that question was found in another old photograph, one of the hundreds in the possession of Mr. and Mrs. Hugo Manieus (Hugo is the son of Ella Mayer Manieus, Emma's sister).

Emma was born in 1888. The Mayer house was built in 1899. Emma moved into the house with her parents when she was eleven. She may have learned some of the tasks and skills of the farm wife by helping her mother make the new house a home. She probably witnessed the drilling of a well and the erecting of the water-drawing windmill that can be seen in the photo. She may have helped her mother cook in the building that the photo shows as separate from the house. I inferred that it was the kitchen because that room was often built apart from the living quarters to contain its heat in summer and to reduce fire hazard.

As I thought about Emma in that home on the day she was wed, I wondered what went on in the kitchen and in the living areas. *What was cooking there on December 10, 1907?*

Mrs. Nielsen had told me that the food served at her own wedding included sweet rice. She said "rice—sweet rice," clarifying her statement to make sure that I understood the rice was sweet. Because other women of the Texas Hill Country spoke to me about sweet rice as a favorite staple recipe and because I had never tasted sweet rice, I asked for a recipe.

Ophelia Weinheimer told me how to make *suesser reis* (sweet rice):

> Cook one cup rice in 2-1/2 cups water. Add 2-1/2 cups milk; cook slowly. When the rice thickens, add 1/2 tsp. salt and 3/4 cup sugar. Continue to cook slowly for a few minutes. To serve, place some sugar and cinnamon on top.

Ophelia prepared the dish for me to sample. As the recipe indicates, sweet rice is more like a dessert dish than a vegetable. Sweet and gently spiced, it is reminiscent of rice pudding, though its texture is creamier.

Reflecting on Mrs. Nielsen's wedding menu, I wondered about sweet potato salad. Ophelia described sweet potato salad as German potato salad with sweet rather than white potatoes. The sweet potatoes are boiled in their jackets, then peeled and cubed. Pieces of ham or bacon are sauteed with onions in a pan. Sugar, vinegar, and salt are mixed with water to taste. This, along with the sauteed bacon, is poured over the sweet potatoes and served as a salad. According to Ophelia, the salad was popular among members of her community. It is reasonable to assume that

The lintel of the Mayer house verifies its owner: F. Mayer. And it tells the year it was built: 1899.

Mr. and Mrs. Ferdinand Mayer and their two sons, Edgar and Hugo, stand in front of the family home in Albert, Texas. These were Emma's parents and brothers. The year is estimated as 1915. *Photograph reproduced courtesy of Mr. and Mrs. Hugo Manieus, Albert, Texas.*

Emma's wedding dinner included sweet potato salad and sweet rice, served in large quantities.

The parlor and porch of the Mayer house must have been crowded with relatives and friends that afternoon of December 10, 1907. Families tended to be large and all members, young and old, would have been invited: the Mayers, the Borchers (Mrs. Mayer's family), and the Beckmanns, including Emil's eleven siblings and who knows how many aunts, uncles, nieces, and nephews. If it was a nice day, some of the guests might have gathered on the L-shaped porch to chat before Pastor Heinrich arrived.

What was the wedding ceremony like that these people came to witness?

Reproduced here from Wilhelm Lohe's *Hand-Agende,* ca. early 1900s, are the marriage vows that would be recited during a Lutheran service in the Texas Hill Country at the time Emma and Emil Beckmann were wed. They have been translated into English from the German and the names of Emma and Emil added by Reverend Arhelger.

> *Emil Beckmann,* will you have and hold this *Emma Mayer* to your Christian wedded wife and show her all matrimonial love and faithfulness in good and evil days, till death do you part?
>
> Then answer: Yes
>
> In like manner I ask you, *Emma Mayer,* will you have and hold this *Emil Beckmann* here present to your Christian wedded husband, and show him all matrimonial love and faithfulness in good and evil days, till death do you part?
>
> Then answer: Yes
>
> The matrimonial allegiance, that you promised each other before God and his congregation, I confirm according to the order of the Christian congregation in the Name of the Father, the Son, and the Holy Spirit.
>
> What God has joined together let no man put asunder. Amen.

The ceremony would have been short. The marriage vows could be recited quickly by a nervous bride and groom. Dinner would be served soon after. And the bride and groom would have departed for their own home before nightfall made travel difficult. *Where did they go?*

The Deed Records of Gillespie County contain the following sale of land by Hermann Beckmann to Emil Beckmann on the fourteenth of May 1908. This document, transcribed from the handwritten copy on file in Volume 17, pages 192–194 of the Deed Records, answered some questions about the farm to which Emil took his bride. I knew where it was located because the Texas State Park Service maintains the farm in its dimensions and conditions as in 1915–1918. I asked: *How did Emil get the land? What did he pay for it? Were there any stipulations about its use when Emil obtained it?* And the deed answers:

> *Hermann Beckmann to Emil Beckmann*
> The State of Texas
> County of Gillespie   Know all Men by these Presents, That I, Hermann Beckmann, of the County of Gillespie and State of Texas for and in consideration of the sum of Twelve Hundred ($1200.00) Dollars, to be paid by Emil Beckmann six years after date as evidenced by one certain promissory note, executed by said Emil Beckmann, of even date herewith, in the amount of $1200.00, payable to the order of Hermann Beckmann on or before six years after its date, at Fredericksburg, Texas, bearing interest at the rate of 5% from the 15th day of May 1911, and providing for 10% additional on the amount of principal and interest unpaid if not paid at maturity and said note is placed in the hands of an attorney for collection or suit is brought on same as collection fees; Payments may be made on said note in amounts of not less than $100.00 and only at an interest payment date, have Granted, Sold and Conveyed, and by these presents do Grant, Sell and Convey unto the said Emil Beckmann of the County of Gillespie and State of Texas, all that certain real estate, lying and being situated in the County of Gillespie, State of Texas, known and described as follows: Two hundred and five and 4/5 (205-4/5) acres of land being 101 acres of Survey No. 7 originally granted to M. J. Trevino and 104-4/5 acres of

Survey No. 5 originally granted to Maria J. Guerrero said 205-4/5 acres being bounded as follows:—Beginning at the stake on the S. side of the Pedernales River at the N. W. Corner of land conveyed to me by F. Sauer and wife by deed dated Dec. 20, 1900, recorded in Gillespie County, Texas, Deed Records Vol. 7 pages 610–612; Thence South 1178 varas to stake in west line of said tract conveyed to me Hermann Beckmann by F. Sauer and wife, for S. W. Corner of this tract; Thence East 1147 varas to stake in East line of said tract; Thence North 818 varas to stone mound on bank of River; Thence West along the River to place of beginning. Provided however that my son Otto Beckmann shall have free access to the water in well situated on South side of premises herein conveyed; the said Otto Beckmann's land being situated on the South side of land herein conveyed and he shall have a passway to said well. A strip of land for a road from the premises this day conveyed to Otto Beckmann to lead by a cow pen situate on premises herein conveyed, and leading to the Austin Road is expressly reserved from this conveyance. Otto Beckmann shall retain the right to cultivate the 12 acres of land now held by him on the premises herein conveyed until the 1st day of January A.D. 1910. It is further understood that Otto Beckmann shall have the privilege to store his crops in houses situate on premises herein conveyed for the term of two years from date hereof. It is further agreed that I the said Hermann Beckmann reserve the right to gather one half of the pecan crop on the herein conveyed premises. To have and to hold the above described premises, together with all and singular the rights and appurtenances thereto in anywise belonging, unto the said Emil Beckmann his heirs and assigns forever. And I do hereby bind myself, my heirs, executors and administrators, to Warrant and forever defend all and singular the said premises unto the said Emil Beckmann his heirs and assigns against every person whomsoever lawfully claiming or to claim the same or any part thereof. But it is expressly agreed and stipulated that the Vendor's lien is retained against the above described property, premises and improvements, until the above described note, and all interests thereon, are fully paid according to its face and tenor, effect and reading when this deed shall become absolute. Witness my hand at Fredericksburg this 14th day of May A.D. 1908.

Hermann Beckmann

Hermann Beckmann sold the land to Emil for $1200 to be paid over a six-year period with 5 percent interest to be paid after the first three years; the interest jumped to 10 percent on the unpaid balance if the loan was not repaid in six years. There were stipulations that Emil's brother Otto (a witness at the wedding) would have water rights, roadway rights, and be permitted to farm twelve acres. It seems, therefore, that Otto would have lived on the same property as the newlyweds during the early years of their marriage. *Where would Otto have stayed?*

The answer was given by Edna Beckmann Hightower, Emma's daughter and only living child. Edna remembered:

> My daddy's family was from Luckenbach, Texas. Opa (German, "Grandpa") Beckmann settled there when he came from Germany.
>
> My mamma and daddy moved into the log house when they were married. Daddy bought the land from Opa Beckmann. There was the log house and the rock house. Mamma and Daddy started out in the log house. Uncle Otto lived in the rock house.

Emil brought his bride to a log house on the tenth of December 1907. It was a four-room structure that had been built by the previous owners, the Sauers, over a period of time; the original log cabin had been expanded by attached rock rooms. The house Emma moved into as a bride was substantially less than the one she had come from.

If Emma was disappointed on moving from her father's Victorian stone house to her husband's house made of logs, one piece of evidence suggests a diversion shortly after moving into the place: they had a chivaree.

35

Emma and Emil Beckmann started their married life together in this log house on a farm in Stonewall, Texas near the Pedernales River. Note the slant of the roof and the way the logs are crossed and chinked. The sloping roof and saddle notching (hollowed-out saddle-like forms on both sides of log ends) are typical of the Texas Hill Country and associated with Germans. Saddle-notching leaves relatively large spaces between the logs to be chinked.

Members of the Albert-Stonewall-Fredericksburg community described pre- and post-wedding events that were part of the hill country tradition.

Vera and Marvin Schuch (b. 1915 and 1913 respectively in Fredericksburg) reported that chivarees were held after dark. Mrs. Schuch said:

> We'd sneak up on them with cow bells. It happened a couple of days to a week after the wedding.

Mr. Schuch added:

> The disc from the old disc plow—they'd beat it with a hammer. What a lot of noise we'd make. After we got the bride and groom up we'd eat and drink lots of beer that was brought by the parents of the groom.

Lina Bauer Uecker (b. 1889 in Albert, d. 1984 in Johnson City) remembered:

Oh yes, the Beckmanns had a chivaree. The day before the wedding they made Emil ride the rail. They made him stay on the fence for about half an hour. He was mad. Didn't like it much.

Reverend Ernst Arhelger told me:

They used cowbells for the chivaree, as many as could be found. Ten to fifteen men would rattle cowbells. They'd carry on the din for thirty minutes, then have food and beer.

What must Emma have thought? What must she have felt when she was rudely awakened by friendly, noisy chivaree-makers?

Emma's Story

UESDAY, *the tenth of December 1907* I can imagine Emma awakening that weekday morning in her parents' house wondering what the weather was going to be like. She snuggled under the covers of the bed she has shared with her younger sister Ella for many years now, knowing that this day marked the end of that sharing. But she knew it was time to rise; thin rays of sunlight were already painting patterns on the floral striped wallpaper her father had so proudly installed. Ella had left earlier to help their mother with wedding day preparations. Emma realized that she was being allowed to stay in bed a little longer than usual on this day.

The cold of the floor was always a bit of a shock when she first got out of bed on these crisp, cool days of early December. The sunlight was a good sign, she thought. Perhaps the weather would be pleasant today. That would make it easier for the wedding guests to travel the few miles that could take an hour or two by horse and buggy.

Emma dressed quickly, enjoying the warmth of her long-sleeved and high-necked shirtwaist and the yards of fabric that made up her petticoats and full-length skirt. Cotton stockings probably felt good; so did the high shoes she laced up around her ankles. She straightened the bed, then pulled on a bulky wool sweater and made her way to the kitchen in the building directly across the way from the house.

Mrs. Mayer and Ella were busy preparing a country breakfast of pork from the smokehouse and eggs gathered the evening before from the nests in the hen house. Summer-made jams had been pulled from pantry shelves to spread on thick slices of bread that held the aroma and taste of yeast. It was a young family that greeted Emma with special recognition that morning in a kitchen scented with sizzling pork and boiling coffee. The parents of the bride were in their forties: Papa was forty-eight; Mama was forty-two. Emma's brother, Edgar, was fifteen. The youngest child, Hugo, was just eleven. And, of course, seventeen-year-old Ella was as excited about the day's events as the nineteen-year-old bride herself. For Mr. and Mrs. Mayer, this was the wedding day of their firstborn—a happy and a sad occasion for sensitive, caring parents.

The family's high spirits warmed the house at least as much as the kitchen stove, and the rising out-of-door temperature promised the refreshing warmth of late fall in Texas and, most likely, a sun-shiny afternoon for Emma's marriage to Emil Beckmann.

Immediately following breakfast, Mrs. Mayer and both daughters started preparing the wedding dinner. Upwards of thirty relatives and friends would have to be fed on the pork Mrs. Mayer was roasting in the oven of her large range. They had done as much as they could during the preceding days. Many loaves of white and dark bread testified to the mixing and kneading and baking that had been the women's chief occupation on Monday. Before that, they had made the cakes. The pantry boasted layer cakes, white with chocolate frosting and cream fillings, mahogany and jam cakes, and rich pound cakes. And even before that, for several weeks, cookies were turned out by the dozens. Ella and Emma were now taking these from their storage places, decoratively positioning the sweet morsels on the family's best china platters. Hugo and Edgar pestered the girls for samples. Until now, they had been denied satisfaction. But today Mrs. Mayer acquiesced, even over Emma's mild protests. Only the sweet rice was left to be prepared a few hours before the ceremony so that it could be served warm at dinnertime. Mrs. Mayer reserved that task for herself. It was, after all, one of her firstborn's favorite dishes—not too sweet, with just a hint of cinnamon. She wanted it to be perfect on this day of all days.

By noon or thereabouts, Emma began readying herself for the wedding ceremony. Ella helped her lace the corset that gave Emma the trim, well-defined waist seen in her wedding portrait. A smooth-fitting petticoat closed perfectly around the nipped-in waist. Emma slipped over her head the camisole she had made for herself and trimmed with Mrs. Mayer's hand-crocheted edging. She buttoned it down the front, then pulled the ribbon that was woven through the crochet-work to take up the slack in the garment, holding it in place with a bow.

The girls were full of chatter. They giggled over the reports their brothers had given them of Emil's "bachelor party" ordeal of riding the rail. They anticipated the chivaree that all newlyweds could expect. *On which night would it come?* They predicted it would occur soon after the wedding day because the Beckmann family lived so far away in Luckenbach that they would certainly want to reduce the number of round trips they made to Stonewall for partying. Some of the Beckmanns would be staying with the Mayers tonight. One more night's stay could be conveniently arranged. Of course, Ella knew but wasn't about to reduce the surprise of the chivaree by telling the bride. She avoided the obvious question by reminding Emma that they couldn't be sure how long the Beckmanns might stay in Albert. After all, this December wedding date had been carefully chosen so as not to interfere with farmers' work. No field needed plowing, no seeds needed sowing, no crops needed tending on a Tuesday just this side of winter.

Mrs. Mayer's full figure now filled the doorway. Her sisters had come to help with the cooking and household preparations. Now she was free to temper the giddiness of excited teenage girls. Her presence changed the process of dressing the bride into a ceremony.

Emma's wedding dress was carefully laid out on the bed. Mrs. Mayer had given the white batiste fabric just the right amount of starch and had pressed it to perfection. The blouson bodice was draped into a stylishly creaseless paunch; the lace-trimmed high collar held its own form perfectly to encircle the slender young neck of its wearer. The unadorned long skirt shouted of never having been worn. The bright whiteness of the fabric was intensified by the slight starch stiffening and the smoothness of line, uninterrupted by inserts or tucks, from seam to seam, from waistband to hem. Mrs. Mayer placed the bodice on her firstborn, adjusting the sleeves and buttoning the garment down the back with the gentleness and attentiveness of one dressing a china doll. Next came the skirt which she hooked into place; then she wrapped a wide satin ribbon sash around the girl's waist. She stood back to admire her handiwork. Ella smiled her approval. Looking at her image in the dresser mirror, Emma blushed on seeing the doll-like perfection of her appearance. The three women exchanged smiles that spoke of their individual appreciations of this moment, at once poignant and exhilarating.

The wedding guests had begun to arrive by horse and buggy or surrey about two o'clock. For some the journey of several miles from their homesteads had taken over an hour. Mr. Mayer greeted them, offering his guests the hospitality of his home while his wife and daughters continued making their preparations.

Emma piled her long thick black hair atop her head in a loose pompadour that dipped over her forehead. She pulled the hair at the sides of her head to the nape of her neck and fastened it there in a bun with several bone hairpins. A queen could not have received her crown with more ceremony than Emma when her mother pinned the headdress of white veiling and wax orange blossoms to her dark tresses.

The subdued conversational sounds coming from the parlor heightened just a bit. The women surmised that the bridegroom had arrived with his family. In respect to Mr. and Mrs. Beckmann, a decade older than the parents of the bride, Mrs. Mayer left her daughters, urging them to be ready for the ceremony that would begin as soon as Reverend Heinrich arrived.

That time came quickly. Reverend Heinrich was punctual. At 3:30 P.M., without music, flowers, or even very much opportunity to make an entrance, Emma Mayer took her place beside Emil Beckmann, positioned just as they appear in their wedding portrait. Flanked by four youthful witnesses representing both families (Olga Beckmann was twenty-two, Otto Beckmann was nineteen, Ella Mayer was seventeen, and the youngest, Max Beckmann, was sixteen), the couple joined right hands in the symbolic handshake and recited, in German, the simple, egalitarian vows of the Evangelical Lutheran marriage ceremony. In a manner of minutes, Emma Mayer had become Mrs. Emil Beckmann. No rings were exchanged; Emma already wore the one Emil had given her when she agreed to become his wife.

Quietly the bride and groom took their places on chairs positioned together in the parlor. Wedding guests approached to give their congratulations and to share a few pleasantries. The women admired Emma's dress and chatted with her about the household she would create in the log house that stood on the land she and Emil would farm. For Emil and the men at the wedding, farming was the main topic of conversation. It was their livelihood and their way of life. They valued the knowledge it gave them and the skills it required. And so they talked about livestock and crops and farm equipment, about building houses and fences and barns, about planting, harvesting, and selling cotton, about the weather and its impact on their partnership with the land. Not much attention was given to the policies of Teddy Roosevelt's administration. Washington, D.C. was more than a far distance from Albert-Stonewall. It was another world.

As wedding guests mingled and talked with one another and the bride and groom, Mrs. Mayer readied her table for dinner with the help of her sister, Ella, and the Beckmann women. The kitchen table was set for as many places as it could hold. Mrs. Mayer put out her best china for the first serving. Emma and Emil sat down to that first serving with the closest relatives. Platters of roast pork, bowls of sweet potato salad and sweet rice crowded the center of the table where guests could help themselves. Thick slices of bread, neatly layered on an oblong platter carved from one chunk of wood, were passed around the table. Black coffee was poured into large cups; some added milk from the earthenware pitchers the Mayer boys had filled that morning after the milking was done. This was a time for sharing stories of personal experiences and a time for thinking out loud about the future. It was a bittersweet time for the Mayers: the parents were no longer responsible for their firstborn daughter, Ella would now be the only girl in the house, Hugo and Edgar would not have their big sister close at hand, Emma was about to assume a new role. Sometimes tears welled up behind their smiles.

Dinner was served in shifts and one group of guests replaced another at the table until all had eaten. The women of the family were kept busy washing dishes between servings, resetting the table, and restocking serving platters and bowls with large quantities of food. No special toasts were made. No wedding cake was cut and served by the bride and groom. The guests enjoyed a variety of rich German cookies and healthy slices of layer cake washed down with freshly ground and strongly brewed coffee. A constant hum of conversation permeated the house—pleasantly modulated voices of women and the men's deeper tones, punctuated now and then by the laughing sounds of children—all in the German tongue, changed somewhat by transplantation to Texas soil. The relatively short December day forced the bride and groom to leave their wedding party before nightfall. So did most of their guests. Buggy rides along dark roads were not encouraged. Those who had come distances too long for a trip home before dark stayed the night at the homes of nearby families. Emil's parents remained with the Mayers. They would have Emma's bed that night. Ella would sleep on a makeshift mattress on the floor of the parlor; the younger Beckmann boys would share sleeping space with Hugo and Edgar Mayer.

But before the guests departed, they gathered on the porch of the Mayer house and in the front yard to say good-bye to the newlyweds. Emil and Emma got into a buggy and headed for the place they would live in nearby Stonewall. Riding to that farmland along the Pedernales River, Emil couldn't forget that he was indebted to his father for twelve hundred dollars.

Dark was about to fall when Emil reined up the horses at the log house that he and Emma now called home. The damp cold of night spread itself over the farm, permeating the house. Emma's first task as homemaker was to start a fire in the kitchen stove. She stood in the chilly kitchen shivering, wishing more for a little romance than a warm house.

Late in the evening hours of Friday, December 13, Emma and Emil were awakened by clattering cowbells and clanging harrow discs. They knew the signal immediately: their chivaree had begun.

Without exchanging a word, the two jumped out of bed to dress faster than they ever remembered doing. And all the time the revelers—brothers and sisters, friends and relatives—were shouting and making a deafening din. Even after Emil had invited the merrymakers into the house, they remained outside, ringing the bells and striking the harrow disks with hammers, murdering the natural silence of nighttime in the hill country. This behavior was in sharp contrast to their gentle and quiet manners at the wedding. Even Emil's parents were in a festive mood—they brought the beer.

Thirty minutes of noise-making seemed to satisfy everyone. By the time they were done, Emma had a fire going again in the kitchen stove and several kerosene lamps lit in the kitchen and front room of the house. Her mother and sister helped her spread out the foods she had stored for this expected event. Secretly, Emma had been looking forward to her chivaree. She loved parties. Her cheeks flushed when, as she stood watching her friends and family members laughing and talking around her table, eating food that she had prepared, she realized that this was her very first try at being hostess and that other firsts were yet to come.

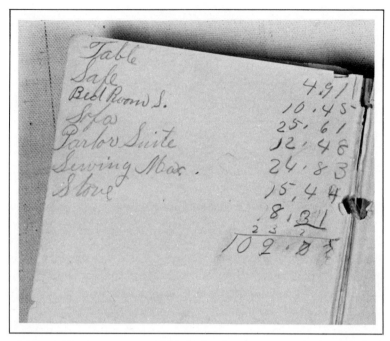

Signpost Artifact Two: Emma's wish list for her dowry, written in her own hand on the end papers of a copy of the 1893 *Report of the Secretary of Agriculture*. Photographed by permission of Mrs. Edna Beckmann Hightower, Stonewall, Texas.

three

The Wish List

RITTEN on the end papers of a stained and yellowed bound volume of the 1893 *Report of the Secretary of Agriculture* is Emma Mayer's wish list for her dowry. In her own handwriting, Emma listed seven items of furniture, with prices, that she wanted for the home she was soon to make as Mrs. Emil Beckmann. The book with its list was given to me by Edna Beckmann Hightower, Emma's daughter. Edna identified the writing as her mother's.

Handwriting samples are always interesting because they can carry clues to personality characteristics or, at least, the feelings that the writer may have had at the time. You don't have to be a handwriting analyst to read determination and straightforwardness in Emma's large clear letters and numbers. She made firm marks with her pencil. The indentations of the numbers she apparently tried to erase are still evident more than three quarters of a century later. The upward slant of her writing is generally thought to reflect optimism—a positive feeling. The curled and interlocking M, a, and c of the abbreviated notation for sewing machine seems playful. Her numbers are large and loose in formation. No preoccupation with precision is evident here. Corrections were made in places as write-overs; in the sum a "9" was made into a "2" and a "7" into a "0." This nineteen-year-old bride-to-be must have been anticipating homemaking with some pleasure.

Emma's choice of furniture is interesting. A sewing machine

seems to have held more importance than a stove. She listed the sewing machine before the stove and at almost double the cost: *What kind of sewing machine was she referring to? What kind of stove?*

Why did Emma list a sofa separately from a parlor suite? You would think that a sofa was part of a parlor suite.

And what did she mean by "safe"? What kind of a safe was she wanting for her house?

The prices Emma recorded for each object are, by our standards, remarkably low. *Where did she find out what these things cost? Were these the regular prices for such objects in her day? Where did people in the Texas Hill Country purchase home furnishings like these in 1907?*

Emma's writing and arithmetic raise questions about her schooling. The style of her penmanship is distinctly different from handwriting styles taught in school today. The 1900 census lists Emma as "at school" and able to read and write. *Where did she go to school? Who were her teachers? What did she study?*

Emma shows us the method of column addition she had been taught. She records the number she carried to the next place at the bottom of the column of numbers to which it must be added. *When was that method of "carrying" in column addition taught?* At first glance, an error appears in her addition: the "3" to be carried from the units column should be a "4." And yet, the sum is correct. Perhaps the apparent erasures indicate the source of the problem. Emma changed the price of the stove from a double-digit dollar figure and some cents to $8.31. *Why?*

The book in which Emma wrote her wish list is one on agriculture. *Whose book was this?* I suspect that it belonged to her father. The 1900 census lists Ferdinand Mayer's occupation as farmer.

What about Augusta Mayer (nee Borchers), his wife—Emma's mother? The census records show her place of birth as Germany. *What type of home did she make for her family—the home in which Emma grew up?* I could better understand Emma if I knew what her childhood had been like and the models she had for woman, wife, homemaker, and mother while growing up. I went back to Emma's wish list for her dowry, intrigued by her selections of home furnishings. *Where did she plan to put all that furniture?*

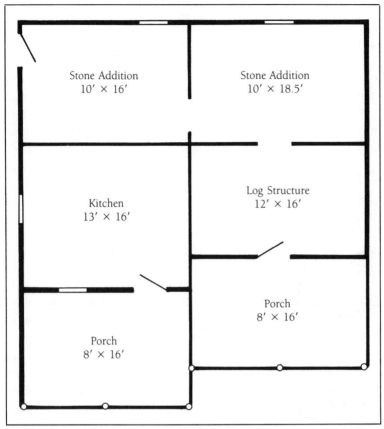

This floor plan of the log house into which Emma moved as Emil Beckmann's bride in 1907 shows four rooms and two porch areas. Note the size of each room.

Portfolio of Evidence

I made a floor plan of the log house with stone additions that Emma moved into as Emil's bride. The four rooms are not very large. I tried to visualize those rooms with the furniture that Emma names on her wish list, only to realize that my contemporary notions of what comprises a bedroom suite, a parlor suite, and the furnishings for a kitchen might not be consistent with Emma's experience in 1908.

In the Sears, Roebuck and Co. catalog of 1908, some pieces

of furniture like those Emma named are listed at prices compa-
rable to those she recorded. She may have consulted a catalog
from Sears, Roebuck or Montgomery Ward when making her list.
Or perhaps she made a day's trip to Fredericksburg to look at and
price furniture that could be purchased there. It seems that she
intended to buy new furniture rather than make do with someone's cast-offs. The fact that she could think in terms of new furnishings suggests that the Mayer family was prosperous. Emma's
parents apparently could afford to outfit their daughter's home.

I could find no back issues of the local newspaper, *Das
Wochenblatt,* that carried ads for furniture—or for many other
things or services, for that matter. No one to whom I spoke remembered fliers or other printed and duplicated ads then like
those that today clutter our mail and increase the bulk of our
newspapers. But everyone remembered having a Sears, Roebuck
catalog. Even if Emma bought her furniture from a merchant in
Fredericksburg, she certainly had opportunities to peruse a Sears,
Roebuck catalog before making her choices. As I looked through
the pages of home furnishings in the catalog, I found a range of
prices for each item in Emma's list. Those with catalog prices
similar to the ones Emma listed must have been close to what she
wanted in style and quality. The slightly higher costs that Emma
noted could be the retail prices of a local merchant or include
shipping charges or merely reflect slight variations in the prices of
things from year to year.

The safe in Emma's list was undoubtedly a kitchen cabinet or
"pie safe" as it was called in the Texas hills. She could store her
stoneware and cutlery in the cabinet to keep them "safe" from in-
sects and accidents in a kitchen outfitted with not much more
than a table and chairs and a stove. That's about all that can fit into
the room, with its built-in shelves, that served as her kitchen in
the early years of her marriage.

Emma's selection of a stove is curious. She seems to have
lowered the price when she made her list. According to the Sears,
Roebuck catalog, she could buy only a simple stove for $8.31. I
wondered why she apparently was willing to have a small stove
when larger ranges were available. Maybe there was a stove in the
log house. Maybe she expected to buy a better one later. In any
event, at the time of making her plans for married life, Emma gave

The Sears, Roebuck and Co. catalog of 1908 contained household furnishings on Emma's wish list: stove, range, bedroom suites, parlor suites, Victorian sofas, and sewing machines.

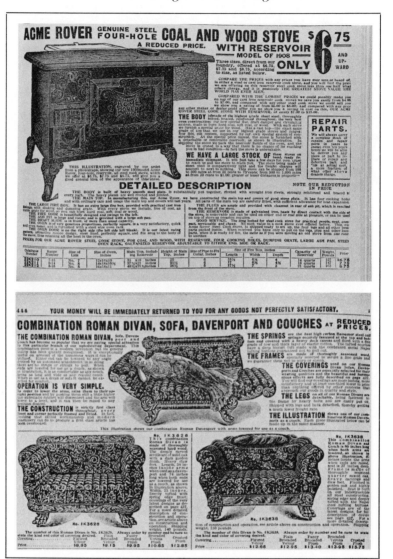

lowest priority to a stove. It holds the lowest position on her list and, judging from the gradations in cost for stoves of her day, Emma allocated a relatively small amount of money from her dowry to buy one.

If cost is an indication of preference, Emma was most interested in outfitting her parlor, although no room in the cabin seems particularly well suited to a sitting room's function. Most of the parlor suites of her day had a sofa, arm chair, and rocker. Emma must have been thinking of a Victorian couch when she listed a sofa separate from the parlor suite. *Did she visualize herself entertaining friends while gracefully seated on that couch, or was she merely following the fashion of the day?*

Emma's bedroom suite most likely included a double bed, dresser with mirror, and a washstand. According to catalog illustrations, those were standard bedroom furnishings at the time. The washstand was a necessity in a house without plumbing. Emma may have had visions of a pretty floral-patterned china washbowl and water pitcher to place on that piece of furniture. (Mrs. Nielsen remembered that the Mayer household was nicely furnished.) The washstand's drawers also supplemented storage space in the dresser—an important commodity in a house without closets. Emma made no mention of a wardrobe. It is unlikely that the bedroom suite she had in mind included one. Perhaps she planned to store her clothing in drawers. Maybe she had a chest to store it at the foot of the bed.

Although Emma undoubtedly expected to become a mother in time, no furnishings in her list suggest that. She didn't ask for another bed for her home, whether for future members of her family or for overnight guests. The extra sofa suggests that she was thinking of sitting room guests; the absence of an extra bed in her list seems to reinforce the idea that for Emma, guests were of the Kaffeklatsch, not the overnight, kind.

And then there's the sewing machine. This must have been an important tool for daily use in the Mayer household. I can see Emma moving the treadle with steady rhythm to sew her wedding dress or help her mother outfit the younger boys. Emma probably liked to sew and knew the significance of a sewing machine for making sheets, pillow slips, quilts, shelf liners, undergarments and outer clothes, including functional necessities like shirts for her husband and aprons and bonnets for herself. No doubt Emma expected to sew a lot as a young bride. I wondered if Mrs. Mayer reinforced that idea by example and in the advice she gave her firstborn as Emma planned her home.

Alma Scharnhorst Nielsen remembers the home furnishings she got as a bride in 1912:

> The furniture for my home was purchased in Fredericksburg. I got two double beds, two springs, a kitchen table, a kitchen safe, eight wooden chairs, a washstand, dresser, and round table. All that cost $100 at the furniture store.
>
> My parents made the bedding. I remember watching them stuff mattresses with cotton in our front yard. They made pillows with feathers and cotton-stuffed bolsters. I also took six quilts to my new home; they had been in the making for several years as part of my dowry.

Mr. and Mrs. Mayer may have made the mattress for the bed Emma and Emil would share. Perhaps Emma helped her parents stuff mattress ticking with the cotton, working out-of-doors in the yard of their new home on the road to Albert.

Emma's dowry totaled $102.72. *Could it be that Mr. and Mrs. Mayer gave her a figure of one hundred dollars to work with as she made her selections? Is that why Emma reduced the price of the stove?* There's no evidence to suggest how many of the items that Emma included in her wish list she actually received as a wedding gift from her parents. In any event, she wanted them. That dowry held clues to how she viewed herself as woman, wife, and homemaker. *Where did she get those ideas? What experiences shaped them?*

In my effort to learn about Emma's rearing, I sought things of her childhood. In the photograph collection of Ella's son and daughter-in-law, Hugo Manieus and his wife Margaret, I found the children's portrait. There is Emma as a little girl with her younger siblings Ella and Edgar. I think I would have known that child's face even without identification by relatives. Emma's face had not changed much in the years that intervened between the making of this childhood portrait and her wedding picture. There was no date on the childhood portrait and, although Mr. and Mrs. Manieus were sure of who the children were, they had no record of what year it had been made. The listings for Ferdinand Mayer's family in the census of 1900 show that Hugo, the youngest of the Mayer children, was born in 1896. That could account for his absence from the picture if it had been taken around 1896, give or take a year on either side. In that year, Edgar, who appears in the photo, was four years old, Ella was six, and Emma was eight. The children in the photograph seem to be close to those ages, certainly not much younger or older.

The dresses on the girls are of the same style and fabric. They have the homemade look of garments cut and sewn with imprecision. Mrs. Mayer probably made them from the same fabric (purchased by the bolt or many yards at a time) and pattern, adjusted for size by a mother's sense of her children's physical forms. Here was evidence to suggest that Emma included a sewing machine in her wish list because sewing was a valued and functional activity for women in her childhood home. Deep hems and drawstring-gathered waists were provided so that the girls could grow into these garments and get several years wear out of them. The same "roominess" is not evident in Emma's high-button shoes. They seem to have been uncomfortable—see how the right ankle is turned slightly outward to avoid placing the foot flatly, squarely in the shoe. Emma's stance is awkward. Perhaps her feet hurt when this picture was taken. By contrast, Ella's shoes seem to have been more comfortable for the child. They look newer too.

Both girls have curls on the tops of their heads, curls that seem to have been crimped into place with a curling iron most likely heated over the flame of a kerosene lamp. Both were wearing identical necklaces. The only other decoration on their dresses is the wide rickrack at their necklines and wrists.

Another photograph in the Manieus's collection—one that caught my eye as soon as it surfaced—shows Emma at perhaps sixteen or seventeen years of age. The child's face was not changed much by adolescence. The same type of rickrack seen in the childhood portrait is the dominant trimming on her clothing—a bit overdone by today's standards. Emma may have made this dress for herself, using trimmings like those her mother favored. It is not surprising that she acquired her sense of what is pretty

The Mayer children in this photo are, left to right, Ella, Edgar, and Emma. *Photograph reproduced courtesy of Mr. and Mrs. Hugo Manieus, Albert, Texas.*

from her immediate role model: Augusta Mayer. For her young woman's portrait, Emma wore a chatelaine watch but no other jewelry—neither necklace nor earrings. (I wondered if the watch had been a gift.) A large flat bow sits atop the dark hair, piled high in a pompadour just as it was fixed for her wedding portrait.

Emma seems stately of form; she may have been gently corseted in this teenage portrait, but that does not mask the plumpness of adolescence. Her wedding picture shows her to be more slender at nineteen, just a few years later. She stands squarely on the ground. Her hands are large and give her an appearance of strength. No gentle demureness is evident here. Rather, Emma has the qualities of robust youth. Her bearing appears self-confident.

Both pictures were made in a photographer's studio; they are so marked. Mr. and Mrs. Mayer's farming enterprise must have been doing pretty well to permit them to take the time and go to the trouble and expense of having these portraits made. They would have had to travel to Fredericksburg with the children, a journey of several hours from Albert by horse and surrey. It would have meant staying overnight—no small task with three young children. The presence of these photographs is an indication of Mr. and Mrs. Mayer's love for their children.

A sentimental and romantic view of the child was popular in the nineteenth century, and Victorians idealized the child. Pioneers saw the child as helper and the hope of the future. Ferdinand Mayer was Texan by birth. According to the passenger list of the ship *Fortune,* Augusta arrived in Galveston, Texas, in 1868, while still a toddler of three years. Both were of German background. Both belonged to the Evangelical Lutheran church, which valued the innocence and the promise of children. Like others of their time, background, and community, Mr. and Mrs. Mayer were probably loving parents who were strict in gentle ways. Emma would have learned about loving from the ways her parents expressed their feelings for her. The learning she acquired in her parents' home about the role of woman, wife, homemaker, and mother would have been shaped largely by her mother's example. The priorities she established for her own home probably developed from those early learnings. But the family was not the only force that shaped Emma's view of herself and her female place in the society of the Albert-Stonewall community. Other

This portrait of Emma as a young woman was probably made around 1904 when she was sixteen. *Photograph reproduced courtesy of Mr. and Mrs. Hugo Manieus, Albert, Texas.*

forces must have included the school, the church, and her peer group.

A photograph of the one-room school at Albert with its teacher, John Merz, and students (ca. 1895) holds some interesting clues to the lives of children in that area at that time. For instance, the two girls at the far right end of the second row may well be sisters, if the pattern and style of their dresses is any indication of one mother's efforts to clothe her children from one bolt of fabric. I wonder if the same may be said of the two girls in the third row and the child who is fourth from the left in the first row? I also wonder why all those hats are strewn about on the ground and window ledge.

At first I thought that the hats strewn on the ground in that picture had been worn to school to hold down the boys' carefully moistened and combed hair or even to be worn for the picture. Maybe they were tossed on the ground because wearing them only served to shade the young faces beyond recognition. Perhaps the hat on the window ledge belongs to Mr. Merz. Then I came upon another class picture taken at another school in the Texas Hill Country at about the same time; all the boys are wearing hats. When I expressed surprise over this, a former teacher and native of the area remarked, "Oh yes, the boys always wore hats to school." I was struck by this because, in my experience, boys have never worn hats to school. So, it seems that the hats strewn on the ground in the picture of Mr. Merz's class were standard attire for the boys. I'll bet that those hats were cast off at the direction of the photographer who wanted the faces of his young subjects fully illuminated by available sunlight.

And then there is Emma. No one remembers which child she is, but careful observers have narrowed the choices to the second or third girl from the left in the first row. I think she is the child seated third from the left in the light-colored dress. The dark hair, closely set eyes and large ears that appear in the identified portrait of Emma at about eight years of age are duplicated in that young school girl. But I have no proof. My one eyewitness, Lina Bauer Uecker (who was a member of the pictured class), could not remember which child was Emma. She remembered the boys who

The one-room school at Albert was the one that Emma attended. This photo-graph of the schoolmaster, Mr. John Merz, and his students was made ca. 1895. Some of the girls seem to belong to the same family. Emma would have been about seven years old when this picture was taken; she does appear in the photo. *Which child is she? Photograph reproduced courtesy of Mr. and Mrs. Hugo Manieus, Albert, Texas.*

were discipline problems, but she was not able to find herself in the picture even though she knew that she was there. Her daughter-in-law thought that the photo might jog her mother's memory in time, but Mrs. Uecker is now dead. I will never know if my hunch is right.

Nevertheless, more pertinent to my detective work are the clues that the picture contains to school and schooling in Emma's childhood. The group is obviously varied in age and numbers thirty-five. There are a few more girls than boys. *What type of instruction did the children receive from Mr. Merz? Was it the same for girls and boys? Was the instruction in German or English or some combination of the two?*

In search of information about school days when Emma was a girl, I asked some of the senior residents of the Albert-Stonewall community what they could recall of teaching and learning in the one-room schoolhouse. I also searched for instructional materials from the turn of the century that could be associated with Mr. Merz and his students.

Reverend Arhelger told me about the Albert School:

> John Merz taught reading and writing in German and in English at the Albert School. He was Ferdinand Mayer's brother-in-law, a scholar in his own right and a strict disciplinarian.
>
> The primary language of instruction was English even though there were only two families in the community that were exclusively English-speaking at the time. Farmers' children grew up on the farm in the cotton patch. But they'd try to have all the cotton picked before school began in September. It was important that the children did not miss school.

Alma Scharnhorst Nielsen remembered her school lessons this way:

> In the sixth grade, we had oral reading. Grammar was in oral and written work. Spelling was another subject we did orally. The students would line up to spell the words the teacher would give. If you missed a word, you were turned down and another student moved up. If you stayed at the head of the line for a week, you'd earn a headmark. Then you went to the end of the line. Spelling words were also written on the blackboard. Sometimes students studied spelling by writing the words on the blackboard.
>
> We did arithmetic problems at our desks and sometimes on the blackboard.
>
> For geography, we'd read the assignment and then write answers on the questions the teacher gave us or that were at the end of the reading assignment in the textbook. We also drew maps. I remember drawing many maps. I didn't trace them. I copied them. All I had was my pencil and a small ruler.
>
> History too was studied by reading the assignment in the textbook and answering the questions at the end

of the chapter. Sometimes history questions were answered on the blackboard too.

We had memory work. We memorized poems and prose selections.

The teacher would call us up to the recitation benches which were in front of her desk. I remember when it was time to go to the front for a recitation, the teacher tapped the bell on her desk one time. That meant that we should rise; the second tap meant to go forward to the recitation benches; the third tap meant to be seated. The same procedure was used for our return to our desks.

In response to questions about teachers and teaching methods, Mrs. Nielsen offered the following information:

One of my teachers was Mr. Tidd from Missouri. He was very strict. He prepared the upper grade children for taking the teacher's exam. He brought his two children to school with him every day.

The older children helped the younger children with lessons. Mr. Tidd's daughter had a class in the back of the schoolroom for the younger children.

Other teachers I had in addition to Mr. Tidd were Miss Price and Miss Bell. All were strict. No teacher I had ever spanked a student though. They kept them in for recess and talked with them. Rarely did anyone have to stand in the corner.

For recess, the teacher tapped a bell one time to rise, then another tap to walk out. Then when recess was over, she rang a larger bell and we marched in.

At recess the boys played on one side of the building and the girls on the other. The teacher was very strict about this rule.

During recess we had a chance to play different kinds of games. There was a seesaw over an old tree stump. Sometimes we played mumblety-peg by throwing a knife into the ground. Our lady teacher played with us. The girls played jacks; the boys liked marbles.

They'd draw a circle on the ground and draw a line down the center and place their marbles along that line. Then they'd take turns shooting the marbles on the center line out of the circle with the big shooting marbles. The shooting marbles were twice the size of the others. The girls also played jump rope. We played High Water, Hot Pepper, and Chase the Fox. Sometimes we pitched washers into a hole in the ground or we'd pitch horseshoes at a pipe stuck in the ground.

School closing was a special day. The children memorized poems and prose selections. There were marching drills and singing. One time someone brought an organ and they played organ music. Sometimes there were speeches. Mr. Tidd's wife came and prepared us for school closing. She took us outside to our playhouse and helped us prepare. School closing was a time to show what you learned to your parents and friends. I never remember receiving a report card.

Intrigued by Mrs. Nielsen's recollection of her school experiences, I searched for a former teacher who could offer a teacher's perspective on schooling in the Texas Hill Country at the turn of the century. Specifically, I wanted to know more about the curriculum, school closing, and the evaluation of student progress, and what Mrs. Nielsen referred to as the teacher's exam. To my delight, I found Mrs. Christine Brautigaum Brodie (b. 1889 in Fredericksburg, d. 1986 in Fredericksburg) living in her own home in Fredericksburg. Mrs. Brodie had taught in a one-room school. After marrying her teacher, both she and Mr. Brodie taught in a two-room school, she teaching the primary grades and he working with the older students. In addition—and this had special meaning for me—Mrs. Brodie had attended a one-room school at the same time that Emma was going to school. Both women were of the same generation, Mrs. Brodie being only a year younger than my historic persona.

Mrs. Brodie began our conversation by talking about her experiences as a teacher:

The school in which I taught was a one-room building with a rock foundation. A heating stove stood in the middle of the room. The teacher's desk was at the side. I taught grades one through seven.

The children recited at recitation benches. I taught all the subjects including physiology and grammar.

Lunch was eaten in the classroom. Children brought sandwiches for lunch in pails. They ladled drinking water from the bucket we kept in the schoolroom. As we had no well on the school property during the early days, the children would have the task of drawing a bucket of water from the well of the nearest farm and bringing it to school each morning. They had other tasks too. There was a wood-burning heater in the school. The children gathered the wood; the teacher built the fire.

Every day began with a pledge of allegiance to the flag. The children recited in unison.

The teacher decided what lessons the children would have each day. There was a curriculum guide from the state that was given to each school free of charge. We used textbooks that were supplied by the state too. The students brought all their own materials to school such as paper or slate and slate pencil. The slate pencil was made like the wooden pencil we use today except that slate replaced the graphite in the center. When the slate wore down, we'd shave away the wood to expose more slate. When I was a girl in school, we had only slates and slate pencils to write our lessons. A sponge or damp cloth was used to erase the slate and the blackboard too. The teacher's blackboard was made of boards painted black. I never knew any other kind in all my years of schooling or teaching. The teacher wrote examination questions for each level in the class on the board, in chalk. The children prepared their answers while the teacher heard the recitations of children at other levels. After one group had been examined in a subject, another group was called. This went on until all levels had been heard in each of the subjects under study that day. There wasn't time each day for the teacher to hear all levels in all subjects. It was the teacher's responsibility to make sure that all children had been instructed in all subjects each week.

We didn't have report cards. I didn't report to the parents about the children's progress. We didn't have homework either, when I was a child attending school or when I was teaching. Many of the parents would help the children review their school work from textbooks at home in the evening but this was not required. The students were expected to learn while at school.

School closing or *Schulpruefung* was a special event. Men from the community would build an arbor on the school grounds. The students' parents and relatives and friends—the whole community—would attend. Each family brought its own lunch to eat on the school grounds during the day's activities. There were drills of rapid addition exercise, poetry readings, and recitations. The children answered the teacher's questions. Sometimes there was music and singing. The children showed what they had learned. Sometimes a photographer came and took pictures of the children and the teacher. That might happen at any time during the school year. Parents would buy a copy of the photograph as a keepsake for their children.

Mrs. Brodie's recollections about schooling were a mixture of her experiences as a teacher and of the earlier days when she was a student attending school like the one Emma Mayer attended, during the same years as those Emma spent in school. Mrs. Brodie told me:

> I went to school at Meusebach Creek. My mother was not formally educated but she was well-read and made sure that all of her children had a good education. My teacher at Meusebach Creek was Emil Sauer.

That piece of information was especially meaningful. Emil Sauer was the son of the Sauers from whom Hermann Beckmann had purchased the farm that became Emma's home on her marriage to Emil Beckmann. I knew that Emil Sauer was a highly respected member of the community. He was born in 1881 and, after teaching in the community for awhile, he studied at the University of Texas and Harvard University, entering the United States diplomatic corps to serve in exotic places. Emil Sauer was only seven years older than Emma and eight years older than Mrs. Brodie, one of his students. That led me to wonder about how one became a teacher in the hill country during the last decade of the nineteenth century. What Mrs. Brodie told me connected with the references Mrs. Nielsen had made to taking the teacher's exam:

> There was summer normal school. The children from surrounding counties would go to summer normal school when they completed regular school at about sixteen years. There was a test for certification that you took upon completion of the course of study. If you passed the test—the teacher's exam—you would be certified to teach the grade levels for which you demonstrated the appropriate knowledge. The summer normal school was state supported and usually held at the local courthouse. The county judge was the superintendent of schools for the county. Each district had its own trustees to whom the teacher reported. I got my voucher for pay from the county judge. I made thirty-three and a third dollars per month when I began teaching; later on I made thirty-five dollars a month.

I asked Mrs. Brodie to tell me about the routines of the school day when she was a student and about the language of instruction and provisions for religious instruction. She reported:

> School started about 9:00 A.M. We would walk to school leaving the house at 8:00 A.M. The school day ended at 4:00 P.M. Our hour's walk home got us there at about 5:00, in time to do some chores before the evening meal.
>
> Lunch was usually carried in a tin bucket—the kind that syrup might come in. When I was a girl in school, my brothers and sisters went to school with me so we carried our sandwiches and fruit for lunch in a basket. The meal was always simple; we drank water with our sandwiches.

Children stayed out of school to chop cotton; their help was needed on farms where the major crop during my childhood was cotton. So, the school months were usually October to May. It was typical to speak the German language at home and with one another at school. Instruction was in both English and in German. During the First World War, German was forbidden on the school grounds.

We had autograph albums. We'd ask our schoolmates and teacher to sign the autograph album which looked very much like the ones young people use today. We also exchanged friendship cards.

There was provision for religious instruction. I remember that the Catholic children were released from school for religious instruction. The Lutherans had their religious instruction after Sunday services.

Mrs. Brodie's comment about the county judge serving as superintendent underscored the importance of that office for public schooling. It seemed reasonable to assume that the county judge's office might contain primary source materials on the county's early schools. A trip to the office in Fredericksburg brought me face to face with hundreds of school registers and volumes of school board minutes, many of which were recorded in the pen-and-ink script of the early twentieth century. I held my breath looking over the school registers for Gillespie County's townships, hoping that I would find one in which Emma Mayer's name was listed as a student. But just as Mrs. Brodie had said in a variety of ways, there were no records from those early school days. The earliest registers on file were from the years past those when Emma was going to school.

Quite by chance, while leafing through a Gillespie County school register, I came upon a register of applicants for teaching certificates. I was surprised to find that John Merz, Emma's only teacher for the years she went to school (1895–1903), was granted a third grade teaching certificate in December 1908 at the age of 59, after having taught for thirty-three years. *What did that mean? What were the standards of a third grade education in 1908?*

In addition to causing me to wonder about Mr. Merz's background of knowledge (which determined the limits of Emma's academic instruction), this piece of evidence emphasized the informal regulation of rural schools at the turn of the century. Mr. Merz had been teaching for thirty-three years without state certification to teach. Being used to the bureaucracy of public educational institutions in my own time, I found it difficult to understand and acknowledge a less formal organization. Although Emma's times were no further removed from me than those of my grandmother, the search for her story was helping me realize how extensive the changes have been in our society over the past century and how thoroughly my concepts of people, places, things, and human experience influence my interpretations of what has been. The ideas born of our personal experiences cannot help but influence our perceptions and, at times, are responsible for how we understand or why we may misunderstand the way things really were.

What was the curriculum of Emma's school studies? According to Mrs. Nielsen and Mrs. Brodie, Emma probably studied reading, grammar, spelling, arithmetic, handwriting, geography, history, and perhaps physiology. Mr. Merz was known for his ability to instruct in German as in English. Indeed, Mrs. Nielsen remembered:

> One of my friends went to Albert where Mr. Merz had a class of German for his students. And my brother attended school there for one year before going to confirmation so that he could learn to read some German.

Mr. Merz most likely taught Emma to read in both languages. He may also have taught German grammar and spelling in conjunction with reading exercises in the language.

In an antique store in Fredericksburg, I found a copy of a German-language reader bearing a copyright date of 1889. Published by the American Book Company as an eclectic German reader for American schools, the book is reminiscent of the well-known McGuffy's eclectic reader series that had been published by Van Antwerp, Bragg and Company. Curiously, the McGuffy readers are not remembered by former students or teachers of rural schools near Emma's home place. Be that as it may, the McGuffy readers are among those in the Texas textbook collection held by the library of the University of Texas at Austin, as are other English- and German-language readers. *What did those readers teach besides reading? What teaching methods did they use?*

Of the several English-language readers I found in the University of Texas library with copyright years in the last two decades of the nineteenth century, the readers of three companies—Barnes, Holmes, and Harpers—seemed representative of the entire sample.

The *Barnes' New National Readers* were competitors with McGuffy's readers in turn-of-the-century schools in Texas and throughout the nation. The preface to the first reader lays out the principles of instruction on which the series is based. Despite the 1883 copyright date on this reader, many components of the instructional method are consistent with present-day views of teaching and learning, with the exception of the emphasis on drill and memorization.

Preface

The authors of this book believe,—

1st.—That the Word Method is the most natural and practicable, because words are representative of objects, actions, etc., while letters, or sounds, convey no meaning to the pupil, and are devoid of interest.

2nd.—That words of ordinary length are as easily learned as short ones, provided they are familiar to the pupil.

3rd.—That frequent "Reviews" are essential to the rapid and thorough advancement of pupils. By this means the words imperfectly learned are again brought to their attention and thoroughly memorized. That these "Reviews" ought to take up the new words in a different order and arrangement, in order to test the ability of the pupil to recognize them in any situation.

4th.—That thorough and systematic drill in "Spelling" is absolutely necessary.

5th.—That the "Script" from which the pupil gets his first and most lasting impressions should be of large size and accurate form, and not of the non-

The *Barnes' New National Reader No. 1* was published in 1883 by A. S. Barnes and Co. in New York. This first page of Part 1, Lesson 1 illustrates the content of reading instruction for beginning readers.

descript character usually found in books of this class. That it should be free from superfluous line and flourish, and yet have grace and beauty. That it should be adapted for both copying and reading.

6th.—That the lessons should be largely "conversational" in style, to cultivate flexibility of voice and to break up the dreary monotone so frequently heard among children.

7th.—That the lessons of a book of this grade should not average more than seven "new words." That all such words should appear at the commencement of lessons, and be familiar to the pupil.

8th.—That "Outline Drawings" of the objects first presented to the pupils should be made in the presence of the class, as it stimulates them to draw, and thus makes easy and profitable the copying of the "Script of Exercises."

9th.—That the school book of today must be beautifully and completely illustrated. That there must be variety as well as excellence, both in drawing and engraving.

10th.—That the exercises must be instructive and the stories interesting and elevating, and that no artificial system ought to interfere with the free and natural use of words.

11th.—That a book of this kind should be suited to the wants of graded and ungraded schools, there evidently being nothing in the one not readily adaptable to the other.

12th.—That every book of this class should contain a collection of brief extracts from standard literature as to be committed to memory.

13th.—That this book is constructed on the above principles.

Many of these principles recognize the learning needs and interests of children: developing motivation to learn by presenting nicely illustrated stories, relating reading to the familiar in the child's experience, and limiting the amount of new material to be assimilated at one time. These principles have stood the test of time and represent the same type of progression used in contemporary readers. The first words presented are those for dog and cat and chair and other concrete things found in the environment of most children. Simple sentences are constructed: "It is a dog." "It is a cat." "It is a chair." The illustrations in the Barnes readers, in particular, are handsome. The slate exercise in the first lesson is typical of exercises in copying which appear in every lesson throughout the series. When I saw them, I immediately recalled what Mrs. Brodie and Mrs. Nielsen had told me about their school activities being dominated by copying exercises. And I remembered that they had both testified to the prevalence of verses for reading, writing, and reciting. The readers had many verses sprinkled through their pages, some with the specific direction that they be memorized. No wonder, I thought, that Mrs. Nielsen vividly recalled writing her own poetry for self-directed seatwork. Children who are exposed to a great deal of poetry which they copy and recite cannot fail to become intimately familiar with its rhythms and rhymes and might be inclined to write their own verses. Perhaps, like Mrs. Nielsen, Emma wrote verses on her slate too. Unfortunately, the writings of many children on many slates have been wiped clean again and again during those early years of schooling in Texas. I can only guess about the thoughts and feelings that Emma might have expressed on her slate during the times she was waiting to be called to recitation.

Perhaps Emma pondered the morals of the stories she read during her school lessons—morals like those found in all the readers I examined. An example is the story of "Miss Cloud and Miss Sunbeam" from the *Harpers' Third Reader* published in 1888. It begins:

> My window overlooks a garden where two little girls play almost every day. I call one of them Miss Cloud and the other Miss Sunbeam. The first makes a great friend of a pout, and twists her lips thus, ⌢ . The other is always making love to a smile, which gives to her sweet lips a pretty curve like this, ⌣ . Can you guess how they look?

The story tells how the girls went to pick bunches of flowers. It continues:

> Sunbeam gave some of her nicest flowers to her mother, and some to her sister. Miss Cloud said that she had worked too hard to give any of hers away—she wanted them all herself.

In the end, Miss Cloud remains generally miserable and Miss Sunbeam is completely happy. The child reader is admonished to be cheerful and giving, like the beautiful Miss Sunbeam, and to make the best of every situation.

The book affectionately referred to as the Blue-Back Speller was well-known in the nation's schools during Emma's school days and was popular in Texas classrooms. A copy surfaced among a friend's collection of her grandfather's belongings. He had attended a rural school in a Polish community in Texas around the same time that Emma was being taught by her father's German brother-in-law. Every lesson contains sentences to give meaningful contexts for the spelling words to be learned; many of those contexts are moral teachings and some state religious doctrine. For example:

> Good men obey the laws of God.
> Careless girls mislay their things.
> Wise men employ their time in doing good to all around them.
> God created the heavens and the earth in six days, and all that was made was very good.

The book also speaks of the value of education, a message sent in words and pictures. The illustrations facing the title page of Webster's speller suggest that fame is derived from knowledge and that the teacher with a background in the classics can lead the novice to the fruits of learning.

Holmes' Second Reader of 1889 contains a handwriting sample that shows letter forms of the same style as those seen in Emma's handwritten wish list. Characteristically, the sample also has a moral to teach. Developing the morality of young people evidently was a prominent educational goal at the turn of the century. And while we would argue that it still is, the morality of

Emma's day was more straightforward and less concerned with shades of gray than the morality of today. Emma seems to have lived in a society with less inherent ambiguity than our own. *What did that mean about growing up female in her time?*

As I perused the textbooks, I was struck by the differences between the boy and girl models in the stories. Good girls are portrayed as sweet and kind, gentle and nurturing. Good boys are industrious, fair, strong, and full of initiative. On page after page, in reader after reader with copyright dates in the 1880s and 1890s, this distinction between the sexes is explicit. I also found many references to what might be considered general Judeo-Christian doctrine about the concepts of a supreme being and heaven. The teachings of the public school readers and her religious training probably gave young Emma a clear-cut sense of right and wrong. She probably grew up with an understanding of the separate male and female roles which left little doubt about expectations for behavior. If the content of the readers had a formative influence on her, Emma must have exercised a strong degree of self-discipline. As I read through those early textbooks, I found that children generally were admonished to exercise self-discipline over the frailty of human emotion but girls, in particular, were expected to be the guardians of morality, to have emotional strength in times of adversity, and to be sensitive to other people's feelings. Emma did not have to wonder about the expectations society held for her. They were spelled out in no uncertain terms on almost every page of the material she most likely read and reread at the school desk and recitation bench.

Emma's wish list clearly demonstrates her manner of regrouping ones and tens and hundreds in column addition. I wondered: *What was the method of teaching regrouping when Emma was in school?* What I found in the arithmetic textbooks of her time surprised me.

Elements of Arithmetic for Primary and Intermediate Grades in Public and Private Schools, by William J. Milne, was published by the American Book Company in 1893. Like Webster's Blue-Back Speller, Milne's arithmetic text enjoyed national popularity. I had expected to find a heavy rote learning emphasis in its lessons. Instead, I found considerable evidence to support the notion that children were supposed to understand what they were doing when performing operations with numbers. For instance, on one page students are instructed to learn the basic addition facts by remembering all possible combinations for a sum: the sum of four may be associated with 2 + 2, 3 + 1, and 1 + 3, the sum of six results from combinations of 3 + 3, 5 + 1, 4 + 2, 2 + 4, and 1 + 5. The instructional idea seems to be to help students see patterns which will help them recall their sums with better understanding than is possible by rote memorization alone. The regrouping of units to make tens and tens to make hundreds is presented on the pages of this arithmetic text with illustrations of bundles of sticks: ten sticks make a bundle of one ten; ten bundles of ten sticks each make a hundred. And this is not unique to the Milne textbook; the meaning of place value is also depicted in other arithmetic texts of the same copyright era. The Milne text gives the following explanation with this exercise in column addition:

1. Add 13, 12, 24, 30, and 14.

    13   Explanation. —In adding, the numbers are
    12   written in columns, units under units, tens
    24   under tens, and it is more convenient to begin
    30   with the units' column. Adding, we find there
    <u>14</u>   are 13 units. 13 means 1 ten and 3 units;
    93   therefore the 3 is written in the units' column, and the 1 ten is added to the tens. Adding the tens, we find that there are 9 tens. Therefore the result is 93.

    In adding, do not say 4 and 4 are eight and 2 are ten, etc., simply name results, thus: 4, 8, 10, 13.

This evidence of the teaching of arithmetical operations suggests that Emma was taught the meaning of regrouping as she learned the process. The sum that appears in her wish list was arrived at by using the method explained in the Milne arithmetic book. Emma added the tens from her addition of units to the tens column, recording them at the base of that column with a number of smaller size. I assume that she understood what she was doing because she had learned the arithmetical operation as a concept, not merely a mechanical manipulation of numbers to arrive at an answer.

Besides reading, writing, and arithmetic, Mrs. Brodie and Mrs. Nielsen referred to geography as a regular subject of study. Both women recalled making freehand drawings of maps—a standard seatwork assignment. The extensive collection of textbooks in the University of Texas library includes *The New Eclectic Series Complete Geography* published in 1896. On the title page, under the name of the publisher, the American Book Company, appears "from the press of Van Antwerp, Bragg and Company." Van Antwerp, Bragg and Company was also the publisher of the McGuffey readers. The American Book Company was also the publisher of the *Eclectic German Readers,* not to mention the Milne arithmetic and several other textbooks of the same period. I resisted the temptation to launch an investigation of the textbook publishers of Emma's school days.

The maps included in the text are so detailed that it would take hours for a child to reproduce one like that of central Europe. It was interesting to note the political divisions of Europe that existed in Emma's childhood. The German Empire and Austro-Hungarian Empire are no more. The principalities that comprised them were meaningful political areas to members of the German community of Emma's heritage. Many of the descendants of German immigrants to the Texas Hill Country mentioned to me that their forebears came to Texas in search of freedom from the strife of long-term border disputes among the principalities of the German Empire. In fact, they told me, the reason that German settlers in Texas opposed the state's secession from the Union in 1861 was because they remembered the problems of a nation divided in the land of their origin.

Emma's geography studies likely included careful examination of the map of central Europe. The textbook's table of contents also lists Asia, Africa, Australia, the Pacific Islands, South America, Central America, Mexico, the West Indies, and North America, with heavy emphasis on the states and possessions of the United States. Emma may never have set foot outside a twenty-mile radius from the place of her birth, but she certainly was exposed to faraway places. In all likelihood, she knew their geography better than even many of us who have visited those foreign lands.

There was more to Emma's school curriculum than I had the time or patience to explore. There were history textbooks—Texas history—and grammars and books in each subject at various levels, each interesting in its own right. In the six or seven years that Emma may have spent under Mr. Merz's instruction, she could have learned at least as much as we typically associate with a complete elementary school education. In fact, if she was a motivated student and her teacher was knowledgeable, Emma could have advanced through secondary school studies. Mr. Merz is the key to understanding Emma's level of education.

Questions about Mr. Merz plagued me as I examined the textbooks. One in particular really bothered me: *Why after thirty-three years of teaching experience and community acknowledgement as a scholar was Mr. Merz awarded only a third grade teaching certificate?* I thought that I could find an answer in the questions on teacher examinations of the year 1908 when Mr. Merz was awarded his certificate. Mrs. Brodie had told me that all students could obtain a teaching certificate upon completion of the elementary course of study and successful performance on the teacher's examination. She remembered taking the teacher's examination in 1905; subsequently, she was certified to teach the elementary grades. I called the Texas Education Agency, but no office there had records of teacher examinations from those early years. The University of Texas special collections library had no record either. In the Texas State Library, the earliest reference on file to the content of a teacher's examination was 1920. A reference librarian at the Texas State Library who got interested in my search came to the conclusion that if such a document existed, it would have to be happened upon by chance in some collection of documents held by someone with an interest or family background in teaching. I was intrigued by this apparent dead end in my detective work. *What was the meaning of a third grade teaching certificate?*

The reference librarian at the Texas State Library uncovered Bulletin 117 of the Texas State Department of Education. Dated April 1920, this bulletin, titled *Examinations and Certificates,* contained the earliest documentation of requirements for and types of teacher certificates in the library's holdings. It lists and describes four teaching certificates:

Second Grade

An applicant for a second grade certificate shall be examined in spelling, reading, writing, arithmetic, English grammar, geography, Texas history, elementary physiology and hygiene, with special reference to narcotics, school management and method of teaching, United States history, and elementary agriculture.

First Grade

An applicant for a first grade certificate shall be examined in the subjects prescribed for a second grade certificate and in addition thereto in English composition, civil government, algebra, physical geography, elements of geometry, and general history.

Permanent Primary

An applicant for a State permanent primary certificate shall be examined in the subjects prescribed for a second grade certificate and in addition thereto the subjects of civil government, English composition, physical geography, the history of education, elementary psychology applied to teaching, and English and American literature.

State Permanent

An applicant for a State permanent certificate shall be examined in the subjects prescribed for a second and first grade certificate and in addition thereto in the history of education, psychology, English and American literature, chemistry, solid geometry, physics, plane trigonometry, and elementary double-entry bookkeeping.

In addition to describing the areas of subject matter knowledge required for each certificate, the bulletin identifies the rank of each:

Rank of Certificates

> Under the law, the holder of a second grade or a perma-
> nent primary certificate may contract to teach in only
> the first seven grades of the public schools, and the
> holder of a first grade or a State permanent certificate
> may contract to teach in any public school.
>
> The law makes no distinction between a permanent pri-
> mary certificate built upon a first grade and one built
> upon a second grade certificate, so far as teaching in the
> different grades is concerned.

It appears that the holder of a second grade certificate in 1920
could teach in grades one through seven, the grade levels represented in most rural schools like the one at Albert in Emma's
childhood. But Mr. Merz was granted a *third* grade certificate in
1908; no mention is made in the 1920 document about that rank.

I called Mrs. Brodie and asked her:

> *What was the rank of the teaching certificate you held?*
> Second grade.
> *What did that allow you to teach?*
> All the elementary grades.
> *What was the meaning of a third grade certificate at the
> time?*
> It was the same as a second grade certificate—for teach-
> ing the elementary grades.

After talking with Mrs. Brodie, I was satisfied that Mr. Merz
must have been certified to teach the elementary grades. If there
was a difference between third and second grade certificates in
1908, it was not substantial. I suspect that Mr. Merz had sufficient
knowledge to give Emma and her classmates a solid primary education in the basic skills of reading, writing, arithmetic, and spelling. He probably also knew and taught some geography, history,
and literature, as well as some English grammar and German too.
Textbooks were available for all those subjects. Perhaps Mr. Merz
was given a third grade certificate because his English language
skills were not as good as his German. It would take some digging
to test that hypothesis.

I knew that Mr. Merz had a German language class at Albert School. Mrs. Nielsen had a brother who was sent to the school from the Blanco area, some distance away, to attend that class in preparation for his confirmation in the Lutheran church. At the time, that church held all its services and ceremonies in the German language. Mr. Merz was considered fluent in oral and written German. Reverend Arhelger confirmed the reports of others. He remembered that reading and writing were taught in both German and English at the Albert School and that all other subjects were taught in English only. Textbooks that were in use in the Texas Hill Country when Emma was a child bear this out: reading books were in German and in English but textbooks for other subjects were in English only.

I can imagine Emma obediently standing before Mr. Merz to recite in English some facts from the geography lesson or to read aloud a passage from the German language reader. I can see her writing, in the flowing penmanship of her wish list, spelling words and sentences dictated by her teacher. She was probably a good student although not a serious scholar—girls were not supposed to be in Emma's day. Her daughter told me that in her later life she did not keep reading materials at hand—no books or magazines or even newspapers. Women's chores on the farm didn't leave much time for reading. But they were expected to be literate, and perhaps most important, they were expected to use the literacy skills they learned in their elementary schooling for housewifely duties: making shopping lists, reading package labels, writing recipes, and perhaps composing an occasional note.

School lasted a full nine months in Albert-Stonewall. Even in a farming community, the German parents of Mr. Merz's scholars valued basic education strongly enough to place their young farmhands in the classroom for most of the year. And each school day was a full one.

Emma's public schooling gave her the basic skills and knowledge she needed for the roles of wife and mother in a rural community. The other important institution in Emma's life was the church: *What impact did the Lutheran church have on Emma Mayer's upbringing and that of other young women in her community?*

Reverend Arhelger told me that the Mayers were active mem-

bers of Trinity Lutheran Church. Soon after Emma was born, the
new parents would have initiated their daughter into the church
with the ceremony of baptism. I could find no reference to Emma's
baptism in the records of Trinity Lutheran Church for good reason, which I did not immediately recognize even as I perused the
limits of the church's ledger: that church was not yet established
in 1888 when Emma was born. So I went to Fredericksburg,
where the oldest Lutheran church in the community still holds
services for its congregation. I found Emma's baptism recorded in
the old ledgers of Zion Lutheran Church. She had been baptized
Emma Lydia Christine on the twenty-sixth day of February in the
year of her birth. The handwritten entry has the aesthetic qualities
of the script of that era, beautiful to contemplate as well as easy to
read. The baptismal record gives Emma's mother's maiden name
as Borchers and shows two of the four witnesses to bear the same
surname. Perhaps Heinrich and August Borchers were Emma's
maternal uncles. Of the two women listed, one carries the Mayer
name; Fraulein Mayer must have been one of Ferdinand's sisters. I
could not tell who Lydia Koch was but guessed that she, like the
others, had a close personal relationship with the family because
the witnesses to a baptism would serve as the child's godparents.
According to Reverend Arhelger, that role carried responsibilities
for seeing to the religious training of the child until the time of
confirmation. These would be trusted people.

What about confirmation: when did it occur? what did it entail?
how important was it in Emma's life?

Back at Trinity Lutheran Church, in the ledger for the first
few years of the twentieth century, I found the entries, in German,
for both Emma's and Ella's confirmation. Both were confirmed on
the fifth of April 1903. My penchant for determining the days of
the week on which ceremonies are held prompted me again to
consult a perpetual calendar. April 5, 1903, was Palm Sunday.
Emma would have just turned fifteen at the time; Ella was thirteen.

Something curious popped out at me as I examined the confirmation records—an apparent inconsistency. They show that
Emil Beckmann was confirmed on March 29, 1907—when he
was twenty-five and just nine months before his marriage to
Emma. The same confirmation date appears for Olga Beckmann,
who was twenty-one years old and would be a witness at Emma

Emma Mayer's baptism is recorded in the ledger of Zion Lutheran Church in Fredericksburg, Texas. *Photographed by permission of Zion Lutheran Church, Fredericksburg, Texas.*

and Emil's wedding ceremony. I could find no reference in this ledger to the older Otto Beckmann, also a witness to Emma and Emil's marriage. Both Olga and Emil were listed as having been born in Luckenbach. *Why were they confirmed so much later in their lives than Emma and Ella?* I needed information about the customs of confirmation in the Evangelical Lutheran church in the Texas Hill Country.

Confirmation is an important rite of passage in the Lutheran church as in other religions. But I needed to find out how it was viewed and practiced by the people of the Stonewall-Albert-Fredericksburg community in the early years of the twentieth century. I asked several people to tell me about confirmation as they experienced it: the preparations, the ceremony, and the celebration.

Anna Meier was born in Switzerland in 1895 and came to Texas with her father in 1906. Her recollections of her confirmation were translated from the German by Ophelia Weinheimer and Hilda Moldenhauer, who were present during my conversation with "Tante Anna" (German, "Aunt Anna"):

I couldn't go to regular school because I was hard of hearing. But I did go to religious instruction on Tuesday and Friday for many months in preparation for my confirmation. That was in 1913.

Pastor Heinrich was the minister at Trinity Lutheran Church then. Until 1904, the Rev. Kupfernagel had been pastor. There were about seven or eight girls and the same number of boys in my confirmation class. Pastor Heinrich explained the doctrines of the church to us and we memorized the catechism. All instruction and reading was in German.

On Good Friday, our examination for confirmation took place at the front of the church. It took about two and one-half hours for the pastor to ask us each the questions on the catechism.

My sister sewed my confirmation dress. It was a pretty white dress. And, on Easter Sunday I rode in a buggy with my parents to church for confirmation ceremonies. Some of the young people went in buggies. We took food along for lunch. We were confirmed at Easter Sunday church services, then we had a picnic lunch and visited with one another. My parents gave me a ring for my confirmation. On the Sunday after Easter, the children who had been confirmed took their first communion.

Tante Anna's testimony gave me an image of Emma preparing for confirmation in a serious way. *What was that preparation like? How long did it last?* Reverend Arhelger told me:

Confirmation involved religious instruction. Pastor Heinrich had a vacation Bible school in Junction School. Confirmation instruction lasted for one year until Palm Sunday. The children had release time from public school to attend religious instruction. That instruction was given in German.

The same people who served as witnesses at the child's baptism served as his witnesses at confirmation. They are the godparents. When the child is confirmed, they are released from their responsibility to make sure that he is instructed in the teachings of the church. Confirmation is necessary before taking communion and being married in the church.

Quite by accident, I discovered that Alma Scharnhorst Nielson had stayed with the Mayer family when she was nearing the end of her religious instruction for confirmation. She told me that it was common for young people living some distance from the pastor who was preparing them for confirmation to stay in or near the home of the pastor during the most intensive last part of the instruction. During some of the time of her instruction, though, she stayed with the Mayers because the Heinrichs had a new baby. I asked her what she remembered of that time, especially staying in the Mayer household, and she said:

> We had six months of religious instruction in preparation for confirmation. Toward the end of that time, we had instruction every day.
> For two weeks I stayed with the Mayer family so that I could go to religious instruction. The rest of the time I lived with Pastor Heinrich's family. My family lived too far away from the church for me to travel back and forth every day. While I lived with the Mayer family I remember Mrs. Mayer kept her house so pretty—she had curtains on all the windows. Emma was still living at home then. I remember seeing her come home riding sidesaddle.
> My godmother gave me one and one-half yards of ribbon for my confirmation. That was a pretty gift. I was always happy to get ribbons.

I was beginning to realize that these religious experiences must have had an important impact on Emma. I tried to visualize her going to religious instruction, studying her catechism, reciting answers to the pastor's questions, then participating in the confirmation ceremony and celebration. But there were gaps in my knowledge. My images of Emma doing those things were neither always clear nor complete. Also, I was seeking the human interest stories that figure so prominently in people's recollections of life's ceremonies. Being assured by several senior members of the Evangelical Lutheran church that confirmation has not changed over the years since their parents' day, I asked Vera and Marvin Schuch about their remembrances of being confirmed. The following summary of their comments includes additions they made when they reviewed the transcript for accuracy:

> A child was usually confirmed at the age of thirteen or fourteen. Instruction for confirmation took place from October to April. Then an examination was given on the Sunday before Palm Sunday. Lots of questions were asked from our studies in the catechism. On Palm Sunday, we had our confirmation ceremony. The boys wore their first long pants. Before confirmation they wore knickers. The girls wore white dresses.
>
> The church services for Palm Sunday were the confirmation ceremonies. Each child received a hymnal in the German language. Sometimes the hymnal was given as a gift with the child's name embossed on the cover. Other typical presents were cuff links for boys and necklaces or handbags for girls.
>
> We had a party at home after the ceremonies. The party was for the child being confirmed and his or her sponsors—godparents for confirmation were the same as for baptism. The idea was that the godparents were released from the responsibility for raising the child in the church, which they accepted at the baptismal ceremonies, now that the child was confirmed in the church. On Good Friday, those who had been confirmed made their First Communion.

Alma Scharnhorst Nielsen's sister, Ophelia Scharnhorst Neffendorf (b. 1905 near Blanco, Texas) remembered her confirmation much as the Schuchs remembered theirs. Then she chuckled and shared with me this recollection:

> During the time of my religious instruction, I went with two other girls from Post Oak to Trinity Lutheran Church where Pastor Lindenberg held classes. Sometimes families got together to help with the transporta-

tion. One family would furnish the horse, another the buggy, and a third the fodder for the horse.

I remember one horse who had learned to stop when another buggy approached. The family that used that horse to pull their buggy liked to visit with people who were passing in the other direction. So the horse learned to come to a halt every time another horse and buggy approached. We got tired of urging the horse on so many times on our way to confirmation classes. That old horse would stop for every oncoming buggy. One day, we decided that we'd cure the horse of his social habit by hitting him with a buggy whip when he stopped. It was a good plan—or so we thought. Our first opportunity came and we put our plan into action. We didn't accomplish what we set out to do, though— at the feel of that whip, the horse reared and tore the harness. What started out as our little joke turned out to be a joke on us. We didn't get to confirmation class on time that day!

Since the confirmation records at Trinity Lutheran Church show that both Mayer girls were confirmed at the same time, Ella must have accompanied Emma on trips to the church for religious instruction—once or twice a week beginning in the fall of the year, then every day during the two weeks preceding the examination for confirmation.

At church, they joined the ten or twelve other students who came from the Albert or Junction schools. Every confirmation class must have been a collection of adolescents of several ages so that the minister had at least a small group to instruct and confirm. Reverend Kupfernagel was in his last year as pastor of the congregation in 1903. He would have given the religious instruction to prepare young people for confirmation. The instruction was in German and closely followed the catechism. Emma must have memorized answers to the questions that Reverend Kupfernagel asked—those questions were standard ones and the answers were verbatim quotations from the catechism. Emma and Ella must have been examined with the other members of their

Group photographs were taken of confirmation classes in the Lutheran church of the Texas Hill Country. This one is from the collection of Mr. and Mrs. Marvin Schuch of Fredericksburg. According to them, it was taken only a few years after Emma made her confirmation. *Photograph reproduced courtesy of Mr. and Mrs. Marvin Schuch, Fredericksburg, Texas.*

confirmation class on the Sunday preceding Palm Sunday, March 29, 1903. I can imagine how tense an experience that was for the teenagers—being questioned by the minister in front of family and friends.

The photograph of the confirmation class that Mr. and Mrs. Schuch had in their collection of family pictures underscores the importance of the ceremony. The fact of a posed photograph of young people in their confirmation finery would be indication enough of the importance of this event in their lives; the group portrait is akin to those made of high school graduating classes. And the pastor's presence in their midst elevates the portrait almost to the status of an official document.

I did not find photographs of Emma or Ella at their confirmation, but other Lutheran church confirmation portraits of their generation suggest that Mrs. Mayer and the girls probably made dresses out of white batiste for the occasion. The style was a standard one: the bodice had a high neck with yoke, perhaps rimmed with ruffles that extended over the shoulders of long sleeves; full skirts were sashed at corset-cinched waists and flounced at the ankles with one deep or several overlapping ruffles. White flat bows topped the girls' heads or decorated long braids. Judging from Emma's portrait as a young woman, she probably wore a flat bow squarely atop her dark hair. It's quite likely, I think, that she and Ella would have dressed alike; their dresses probably were cut from the same bolt of cloth using the same pattern.

Although the clothing worn by the boys in the confirmation group portrait is not easily discernible, they all sport the starched white detachable men's collar, attached to their shirts with collar buttons, and bow tie that were probably as much symbols of their newly acknowledged manhood as the long pants they must be wearing for the first time. An interesting aside is that the photographer's backdrop was not quite wide enough for the room or the group, although it is a wide backdrop of the kind that appears behind Emma and Emil in their wedding portrait. The photographers of the Texas Hill Country apparently did what they could with the materials they had.

The Mayers had the reputation of being a church-going family. Therefore, the religious and social significance of their confirmation day would have been impressed upon the girls by their parents and their godparents. The girls probably received gifts from each, perhaps a hymnal, a ring, or a necklace to mark the day as one to remember and cherish.

It was increasingly apparent to me that the religious instruction given the youth of Emma's community by the pastor of the Evangelical Lutheran church and the activities that celebrated learning and believing in the principles of the faith were important in the process of growing up there. My information indicated that the Mayers were faithful parishioners at Trinity and suggested that when Emma and Emil married, she would have felt a responsibility for bringing Emil into the church community. That would have been a likely duty for her even if Emil had been an active member of another Lutheran church in the area; there was none in Luckenbach. After all, she had grown up in the Albert-Stonewall community that was served by Trinity Lutheran. And she was not leaving the community to reside near her in-laws.

Emil was moving to Stonewall. Indeed, his father had intended that when he purchased the land by the Pedernales River to which Emil brought his bride.

But there seems to be more to the matter. Emil wasn't confirmed until the year of his marriage to Emma. His sister Olga had not been confirmed earlier either. The Beckmanns seem not to have been regular churchgoers; the children would have been confirmed by the time they had reached fifteen if the family participated regularly in church services. Emma must have been responsible for bringing Emil into the religion; he and his sister were confirmed in preparation for the wedding, since confirmation is a necessary prerequisite to marriage in the Lutheran faith.

I felt safe in assuming that Emma had promised her hand to Emil Beckmann several months before March 1907, because a length of time was needed for religious instruction in preparation for confirmation. Just prior to that promise, courtship activities must have dominated Emma's young life. *What were they like?*

No one I've interviewed in the Albert-Stonewall-Fredericksburg area remembers how Emil and Emma first met. I couldn't help but wonder about that. *What did young people in their day do for fun? Did they have dates? What were the courtship practices in Emma's community?*

According to the testimonies of people of different generations in the Texas Hill Country, courtship practices were remarkably stable over the years.

Reverend Arhelger recalled play parties and dances:

> Play parties were very popular. The young people would be invited to the home of one family, then another, and another so that each month there might be several play parties to go to. About twelve or a few more young people would be at a play party. They'd take all the furniture out of a room and play partner games like "Four in a Circle" and "Skip to My Lou." These play parties were a way for boys and girls to get together. While the young people played games, their parents visited.
>
> There were public dances at Stonewall on Saturdays. They were held in Burg's Hall—the large building had a good space for dancing. There were always young

men in the community who played musical instruments and could make up a band to make good music for the dancers.

Mrs. Nielsen remembered attending the dances:

On a rainy evening, the wooden floor of the dance hall became covered with dirt. The men used cotton hoes to scrape the dirt off the floor after several dances. There would be fifty to seventy-five couples at least attending a dance. Those dances were an important part of courtship in the hill country communities. After dark, the hall would be lighted by kerosene lanterns. And at midnight, a young man could take his girlfriend to lunch. Tables were set up away from the hall in another building. Mrs. J. P. Burg served a fine meal family style for twenty-five cents: sausage, cole slaw, potato salad, homemade bread, and coffee.

If young ladies had traveled a long distance to attend the dance, Mrs. Burg would let them use the upstairs in Burg's store to change into their good clothes. The store was also open on the evening of a dance so people could buy whatever they needed. Mr. and Mrs. Burg operated this business—a store and dance hall—with the help of their older children.

Before I went to dances, young men would come for their dance dates with an extra horse and sidesaddle for the girl. My partner came with a buggy. He often brought a lap robe for me. Some young people walked to the dance if they lived close enough. Maria Nielsen Behrens, my husband's sister who lived near Emma, always walked with her brothers to the dance.

We had party games and house dances too. These were usually weekend games at somebody's house for the young people. We'd take all the furniture out of a room in the house so we could square off and dance games like "Skip to My Lou" and "Four in the Circle." These were English-language singing games—everybody recited the lines as we played.

The candy-breaking was a way we selected partners. We would break peppermint stick candy into lengths so that each stick was broken differently. The halves were separated, boys selected from one pile and girls from another. We matched those pieces of candy to get partners for the dance. If the pieces matched, both the boy and girl could keep the one they drew. Otherwise, only the girl could keep her piece of candy.

Sometimes we would have music at the house dances if there were young people in the group who could play. A harmonica was good accompaniment for the dances.

The play parties took place in the afternoons. Boys rode on horseback to visit girls on Sunday. Sometimes they would go out-of-doors in the good weather. We'd hang lanterns from trees and have refreshments after sundown. The parties usually ended by midnight if there was a full moon that would light the way for people to ride home.

Marvin Schuch seemed to enjoy talking about the parties he went to as a young man: he sang some verses for me when recounting his experiences with partying.

Play parties were times for meeting and courting. We'd dance, play games, and drink lemonade. Sometimes there were twenty to thirty people playing. We played games like "Promenade the Hall" (like a square dance) and "Coffee Grows in the White Oak Tree." Dances were played in the moonlight because there was no other source of light. People sang. I remember "Four in the Middle":

> Six in the middle
> And you'd better know how,
> Eight in the middle,
> And you gotta get out . . .

For the house dances, we'd take all the furniture out of a room. Someone usually played the accordion. Other games we played were "In and Out the Window" and "Drop the Handkerchief."

We had house dances when somebody in our community had a birthday. This happened about four or five times a year. We went to the person's house in a group to surprise them. Then usually we had a house dance or a play party. Everybody took something along to eat like cake, cookies, or sandwiches. Then at midnight we cooked coffee and everybody ate a snack before we went home.

Mrs. Schuch added:

Friendship cards were popular among young people. We'd send little cards to one another that carried messages of friendship. Valentine cards were especially popular. These expressions of friendship were an important part of courtship when I was young.

We also chose a quilt block pattern and gave it to our friends to make one. It usually was a pattern where you could embroider your name and birthdate. Then when you got enough blocks, you put them together and made a quilt. It made a very nice remembrance. I still have mine, fifty years old or older.

Those recollections raised new questions. Mr. Schuch sang all the play party songs that he remembered in English. I asked him about songs in German but he could remember none. He was sure that German was not the language of the songs even though it was the language of conversation. But then Mr. Schuch was of the generation after Emma's. *Did she sing and dance to German songs?*

Vera Schuch's reference to friendship cards also made me wonder about the language. According to Mrs. Schuch, English-language cards were most frequently used even though it was possible to find cards in German. *What would have been the language of the friendship cards that Emma might have received?*

Everyone I spoke with in the hill country remembered singing English-language songs at play parties; nobody remembered German-language songs. And everyone remembered that "Skip to My Lou" was a favorite. It apparently remained so across generations. When I found the verses to "Skip to My Lou," they impressed me as rural: flies in buttermilk, a little red wagon, "purty" for pretty. For the teenagers of rural German Texas, the game was probably more important than the lyrics: like other circle games, it encourages much changing of principals and partners from start to finish. "Skip to My Lou" is a good mixer that is rhythmic and repetitious and easy-to-learn. Its popularity among young people in the German community of the Texas Hill Country, taken together with the popularity of other "Anglo" folk songs and dances, speaks of cultural assimilation. Emma and her parents spoke the German language and practiced German customs, but the ways and language of frontier people from other ethnic backgrounds entered their lives. They must have been growing up in a community that respected its multicultural heritage—a tapestry of customs and traditions shared by farming and ranching people.

I reasoned that German-speaking young people in a German-speaking community would exchange German-language friendship cards. Yet, the more I searched for them in the turn-of-the-century collections at antique shows, in flea markets, in antique shops, and even piles of junk inside and outside stores, the more frustrated I became.

Mrs. Nielsen had saved several friendship cards from her girlhood. It was a common practice, she told me, for girls and boys to have their names printed under the decorative cover of the friendship card. Most carried English words or phrases to express some sentiment. The elaborate illustration is typical of Victorian romanticism: a heart surrounded by lilies of the valley, petals of a rose showing concern for detail, two hands touching gently and demurely, and the single word "Devotion" written in the script of an era concerned with aesthetic appreciations.

Mrs. Nielsen also showed me a valentine card that her mother had received from her father in the 1880s. It too is in the English language. Its ornate paper cutout cover is illustrated in the romantic style. Under that cover is this message:

Friendship cards like this one bore words and phrases in the English language.
Although the card is only four by two inches in size, it is cluttered with decoration.

A Lover's Plea

Thy love is the one thing
        To fold my heart in bliss;
Plight it with a ring
        Seal it with a kiss!

Love me as I love,
        Then will earth be bright,
And the skies above,
        Beam with fairer light!

Love me as I love,
        Give thy heart for mine,
And trust forever more,
        Thy faithful Valentine.

This valentine card was given to Alma Scharnhorst Nielsen's mother in the 1880s. It too is in the English language. *Photographed by permission of Alma Scharnhorst Nielson.*

All the evidence suggested that Emma and Emil conversed with one another and their family members and peers in German. But English was the primary language of instruction in school. English was the language of play party games and friendship cards. English was the language for reading just about everything except the Bible and catechism. For adults, it was the language in which checks were written. It was the language of instructions on dress patterns and embroidery and even many of the ads in the German-language newspaper. Emma and Emil's community was thoroughly bilingual.

Emma's Story

EDNESDAY, *November 20, 1895*
It was the day that a school picture would be taken. Mr. Merz had told all the children in the class to come to school dressed in Sunday clothes. The photographer was going to take a group picture beside the school house; Mr. Merz wanted all his students to look their best.

Mrs. Mayer was looking forward to having a picture of her oldest child with her first school class. It was still dark outside on this morning in late fall. Mrs. Mayer had turned up the flame in a kerosene lamp, as much for its heat as its light. Emma knew what was coming. She hated it because it took so long and, she thought, it made her look so awful. But obedient daughter that she was, Emma responded without argument to her mother's direction: she sat down on the chair Mrs. Mayer had positioned near the table that held the kerosene lamp. Mrs. Mayer carefully combed and parted Emma's hair, then proceeded to wind sections around the heated rod of her curling iron, holding the clamp down against the wound hair and waiting a moment before slipping the iron out from the curl it made. Sometimes her grip would falter and the hot rod touched Emma's tender skin around her forehead, just long enough to leave a pink mark and draw a few tears. Emma was relieved to be set free when her mother was satisfied that the curls were in place. She bounced from the chair, picked up her slate by its handle and the reading, spelling, and arithmetic books that were bound together by a leather strap. These she held with one hand; in the other she carried the pail that once had held syrup and now contained her lunch. Mrs. Mayer watched the child trudge off to school. It would be almost an hour's walk for the little girl but she was sure to meet schoolmates along the way. Their company would make the distance seem shorter than it actually was.

Emma met several schoolmates along the road to Albert School. Some were older than she. The older girls were inclined to take a "big sister" attitude toward the younger children, one that was simultaneously directive and protective.

When they got to school, Mr. Merz was waiting. The children automatically tempered their boisterous behavior which, though quite acceptable on the road, would not be tolerated at school. Everyone knew that. Mr. Merz looked at them in his characteristically stern manner as they quietly shuffled into the one-room schoolhouse. They hung jackets and sweaters and hats on the hooks by the door. Lunch pails and baskets were placed below the hooks, in a tidy row on the floor. Emma took her place at a wooden desk near the front of the room where the youngest children sat. Gently, she placed her books on the bench beside her and her slate on the slanted desk top. Then she waited for instructions from the teacher.

Mr. Merz was facing the children in his usual pose: his right hand rested firmly on his desk, his left was in his pocket. By standing at the side of his desk in that manner, he could see around the stovepipe that channeled smoke from the wood-burning heater in the center of the room straight up through the roof. When all were in their seats, he tapped a small bell on his desk. Everyone rose and, without direction, faced the American flag that draped from its holder on the wall to the right of the blackboard. Emma knew the pledge by heart. She recited it with confidence, though some of the words were merely collections of sounds she made with her tongue. She didn't really know what they all meant. She had some idea of their collective meaning so she didn't ask for an explanation.

Mr. Merz motioned to the water bucket. Immediately, two of the older boys rose to tend to the task of getting a bucketful of drinking water from the nearby farm. If it had been a few degrees colder, the boys would have had to carry in wood for the stove too.

Mr. Merz tapped the bell on his desk again and motioned to the youngest children in the class. Emma and the others in their first year of school rose. Mr. Merz tapped the bell a second time and they moved forward to the recitation benches located just in front of the teacher's desk. He tapped it a third time and the children sat down on those benches. One by one, the children recited their lessons from the appropriate textbook. Emma had not yet gotten used to her teacher's formal demeanor. He was like that all of the time, even at family gatherings. Her knees felt a little weak when she stood to read from a page in her reader. She gulped, then began reading. She found it necessary to pause several times to catch her breath, made short by her anxiety. But she got through the recitation to her uncle's apparent satisfaction. He did not require her to repeat any parts. This done, the teacher gave the children an assignment to be completed under his watchful eye. It was a spelling task—a slate exercise. The children copied on their slates the words their teacher had written on the blackboard. One by one, he checked their work for spelling and handwriting. He wasn't satisfied with the form of Emma's letter "b" in the word "baby." She kept writing the word until Mr. Merz approved. She was glad she had when later that morning the entire class participated in a spelling bee and he asked her to spell "baby."

When the reading and spelling were done, Mr. Merz sent the youngest children back to their seats with an arithmetic assignment. As he had done to call them forward, he tapped the bell to signal time to rise from the recitation benches, time to return to their desks, and time to be seated. Emma opened her arithmetic book to the page she had been assigned. There were several addition facts written there that she was supposed to commit to memory. So she began writing them over and over again on her slate, then wiping it clean and starting again until the sum was automatic. That was the way she saw the older children commit sums to memory. It worked.

By the time Emma was finished doing her sums, Mr. Merz had called the oldest children in the class forward. Emma listened with interest. The children were answering questions from the geography book. *What ten states comprise Central Europe? What states bound the German Empire? What three mountain ranges are on the Austrian boundary?* Those place names sounded strange to her.

When it was time for arithmetic drill, the older chilren were assigned to help the younger ones at the blackboard. Emma liked the big girl who tutored her in doing sums. Christina was kind and treated Emma like a little sister. The younger child enjoyed that; she had to be the big sister at home and, although she liked the privileges of the role, it was a nice change to be treated like "the baby." Emma wrote the combinations she had been memorizing earlier in large white chalk numbers on the place on the lower part of the blackboard where she could reach. It was the same place that many other children before her had been able to reach too. The black paint had been worn off in spots by repeated rubbings with a damp cloth. Emma avoided those bare spots. Some others didn't. Out of the corner of her eye, Emma could see one of the boys filling in the worn spaces with chalk dust. He kept rubbing the chalk stick over the bare wood while his older tutor was looking over another child's work.

Emma knew what was about to happen and wondered why the boy even thought to try such a silly thing. Mr. Merz, who had been at the other end of the room, now began walking in that deliberate heavy-footed way of his toward the boy who was chalking the board. Emma pretended to be looking directly ahead at the board but strained her eyes to see what was taking place just a few steps from where she stood. Mr. Merz grabbed the boy's hand—the one holding the chalk—removed the chalk from his grasp, escorted him to the recitation bench directly in front of the teacher's desk, and sat him there. Emma heard the stern voice, thick with German accent, tell the boy that he would eat his lunch at the bench and stay in during recess. The empty feeling in Emma's stomach told her that any minute now Mr. Merz would instruct the class that it was time for lunch. She was glad that she wasn't the one who would have to stay in during recess on so beautiful an autumn day. Her legs were aching to run.

But no one was permitted to eat yet. The photographer had arrived. Emma and the children knew him as Mr. Benner from across the Pedernales. He often took pictures of people on special occasions. Now they would have to wait to eat until Mr. Benner had set up his equipment and posed everyone for a group picture. Emma's heart sank. That could take hours, she thought. Obediently, the children filed outside to watch and to wait.

Emma watched with interest as Mr. Benner set up his tripod and the large wooden box he called his camera. She had seen cameras like this before in the photographer's studio in Fredericksburg where her parents had the children's portrait made. Having your picture taken was a long and drawn-out process. It was too serious a business for Emma's likes.

Mr. Benner began lining up the children in front of the outside wall of the schoolhouse. With Mr. Merz's help, he arranged several recitation benches in rows. He had the biggest boys stand on the bench nearest the wall. In front of them, he placed the next tallest children. He continued to position the children by relative size so that the smallest ones were at the front. Emma and her classmates, being the youngest, comprised the front row. They were seated on the ground in front of everyone else.

The boys had been instructed by Mr. Merz to place their hats on their heads. Everyone sat or stood very still as directed by their teacher and the photographer. The sun was now directly overhead; Emma felt the top of her bare head getting warmer with each passing minute. She wished she had a hat and secretly envied the boys.

Mr. Benner ducked under the black cloth attached to the back of the camera; it draped over his shoulders. Emma thought he looked funny: a headless body. She wondered what he saw in his big box underneath that black cloth. With darting movements, Mr. Benner's head reappeared just long enough for him to give the command: Hats off! One of the bigger boys lifted his off his head and spun it toward the ground. The hat hit on its side, rolling for a few feet, then spun around once on its brim and flopped down on the ground right side up. The other boys followed suit to enjoy the sport of rolling hats. Mr. Merz allowed this to go on for a minute until he called everyone back to attention as he placed his own hat jauntily on the window ledge. Mr. Benner took another look at the group from under the black cloth. He was satisfied now that all the young faces were in view.

The photographer admonished the students to stay very still. He darted under the black cloth once again, then reemerged into everyone's view. This time he stood with the shutter bulb poised in his hand, gave it a quick sharp squeeze, and announced that a photograph had been made. Emma was glad it was over. She felt hot sitting in the noonday sun, and by now she was starving.

To everyone's relief, Mr. Merz announced lunchtime. Emma got her lunch pail from among the others on the schoolhouse floor and joined the girls of her own age under a large live oak tree that had been on the school grounds long before there was a school there. Emma liked to look up through its branches, to trace the patterns those branches outlined against the sky. Now a friend plunked herself down next to Emma, distracting her from her skywatch. The two chattered about the games they would play at recess as they gobbled down the thick sandwiches their mothers had made for them with homemade bread and slices of cured and smoked ham. Emma found two molasses cookies at the bottom of the tin. Their strong sweet aroma permeated the tin; they had been baked that morning. Emma's friend caught the scent and wished. But Emma saved her none.

Mr. Merz always allowed the children time to play during the lunch break. Today as every day he reminded the girls to play on one side of the schoolhouse and the boys to play on the other. He enforced that regulation without exception. He was equally strict about boys and girls staying clear of each others' outhouses. That made those places all the more intriguing for some. Emma didn't understand why the older boys, in particular, violated that rule so many times.

The shouts of the girls choosing sides for a game of jump rope got Emma's attention. She ran to join them, but being the last to arrive, she had to be satisfied being an end, holding one end of the rope until someone missed. She was determined that when her end was taken by another she'd remain in the line of jumpers until the game was over. She wouldn't miss, she resolved. The girls played "High Water" first. Obligingly, Emma held her end of the rope at the level signaled by one of the older girls who wanted to clear the rope at a height higher than any of her friends had successfully scaled. When they got the rope to a height that none could clear, they tired of the game and began another. This time, the older and stronger rope-turning ends almost wrenched their arms from the sockets as they cranked the rope at breakneck speed for a game of "Hot Pepper." Emma couldn't handle that; she couldn't jump fast enough to prevent her feet from getting tangled in the rope. She tried and stumbled. The ends, heady with a sense of their power over the younger ones, egged Emma back for another try. This time, the rope slapped at her ankles. She went down on her knees. Tears welled up and almost spilled out. The bell calling the children back to their lessons helped her save face, diverting everyone's attention away from her. Emma was trying to act grown up. She had learned by observing the older girls that it wasn't good to show feelings of pain. She dusted herself off and calmly walked back to the classroom as if nothing had happened.

That afternoon, Mr. Merz instructed the children in German. Each age group read from a German-language reader. Emma knew that the older students were preparing for confirmation. That was several years away for her; she didn't think about it very much. But she liked to listen to the older children reading aloud in German. She didn't understand everything she read in her German reader, but she understood the stories that the older students read aloud. It was like hearing her mother speak. In fact, Emma felt more at ease with German than with English. English was the language of school and German that of the church and home.

Every year on the day of school closing, Emma recited her lessons in English just as everyone else did. Her very first school closing in May of 1896 was as exciting as a party. Emma had a new pink dress for the occasion. The pastel hue complimented her dark hair and eyes. A large pink bow dressed the sections of hair that had not been victimized by Mrs. Mayer's curling iron. Emma sat quietly with the other children under the arbor some of the fathers had built for the occasion. She was aware of her parents' eyes trained on her, watching her from their seats behind the rows and rows of benches where the children sat. She fixed her eyes on Mr. Merz; he was speaking to the parents who had come to see and hear their children demonstrate what they had learned that year. Mr. Merz was explaining the day's schedule: first there would be a spelling bee, then poetry recitations followed by readings of original prose and verse writings by members of the class. After lunch, those assembled for school closing would be treated to a play performed by members of the class. The day's events would close with the children singing songs they had learned in school.

At a signal from Mr. Merz, Emma lined up with the other children for the spelling bee. Mr. Merz stood before them, his usual stern expression masking the affection he felt for these children, some of whom he had already given several years of academic and social nurturance. He began delivering the spelling words. First one, then another, and another. He was moving down the line quickly. The students were spelling the words he gave them with ease. Emma's stomach had tightened when she first stood in line. Now that her turn was only two students away, her throat felt dry. She tried to swallow but something seemed to be lodged in her throat. Then it came: her word was "baby," the one she had written again and again on her slate. When she was writing it, she was sure that she'd never forget it. But now her mind went blank. Emma looked at Mr. Merz, then at her mother and father who were waiting expectantly for their firstborn, their first child to go to school, to perform well in front of the neighbors. Mr. Merz pronounced the word again, this time slowly and more deliberately than before, stressing in his German accent, the letter sounds. Emma felt that he was trying to help her. In response, she mumbled a "b," then an "a," another "b"—a long pause—then a "y." Mr. Merz smiled. Mr. and Mrs. Mayer smiled. Emma felt numb. She dared not relax. There would be another word to try to dredge up from her memory as the second round began.

Reciting a memorized poem provoked far less anxiety. Emma had studied the poem over and over with her mother prompting her at home. She knew that she knew it. She knew that her mother knew that too. She was confident that her memory would serve her well. And when her turn came, it did. She recited verses

from the second reader that Mr. Merz had assigned to her by
midyear:

> Work while you work.
> Play while you play;
> That is the way
> To be happy and gay.
>
> All that you do,
> Do with your might.
> Things done by halves
> Are never done right.
>
> One thing at a time
> And that done well,
> Is a very good rule,
> As many can tell.
>
> Moments are useless
> Trifled away,
> So work while you work,
> And play while you play.

Mr. and Mrs. Mayer nodded their approval of both Emma's recitation and the meaning of the words she spoke from memory. Mr.
Merz was satisfied too. Emma relaxed for the first time since the
day had begun. With the grip on her stomach loosened, she could
feel the gnawing emptiness of hunger. She could soon partake of
the festive lunch her mother had packed for the family to enjoy
together on the school grounds that day, beside other families
with their "scholars." She knew that other parents would be talking with hers about the children's performances. While the adults
talked, she would be enjoying the sweet reward of iced sugar
cookies so big that each filled the palm of her hand.

At Mr. Merz's direction, the children joined their parents for
lunch. As if by his decree, the sounds of the German language
suddenly replaced those of English which had just moments earlier dominated the proceedings. Emma shifted easily from formal
English to conversational German. It was the language she spoke
at home. It was also the language of her catechism.

On Palm Sunday of 1903 at Trinity Lutheran Church, Emma and Ella Mayer took their places among the other young women in white and the young men in their dark suits with long pants. Emma was now fifteen. Her schooling had been completed that same year with Mr. Merz's decision that she had learned all he could teach her. Throughout those eight years of schooling, Emma had received religious instruction in preparation for this day. Now, with the entire congregation as witness, Emma sat with her peers in the front pews of the church, listening attentively to the Reverend Kupfernagel's sermon about the importance of this rite of passage, this elevation from childhood to adulthood in the eyes of the church and the community. Both girls sat straight and tall in the hard pews. Their corsets helped to remind them to hold their backs straight. Their white batiste dresses with full skirts bordered by deep ruffles—made from the same pattern—encouraged daintiness. With her sister and the other young people, Emma rose from her seat when the pastor instructed them to do so. She bowed her head to accept the final benediction. Now, in the eyes of the church and community, she had become an adult. She would take her First Communion on Easter Sunday. The next major event in her life would be marriage. Emma knew this but didn't dwell on it. The celebrations of the day remained to be enjoyed in their own right.

After the ceremonies, Emma and Ella joined their parents, other family members and godparents—the same who had witnessed their baptisms—for a Sunday picnic lunch. It was like most Sunday picnics on the church grounds, with one difference: the girls were the center of attention this Sunday. Emma relished every minute of the attention. The occasion was an especially happy one because everyone viewed it as a milestone—one that every child in the community was expected to achieve. The expectations were clear and Emma knew beyond any doubt that she had attained them.

Emma knew, of course, that there would be gifts. She wondered all through lunch what they might be. She had some idea but wasn't sure. After the cured sausage had been eaten with thick slices of white bread spread with peach jam made the summer before, Mrs. Mayer gently lifted out of the basket in which she had packed the Sunday lunches a beautiful layer cake frosted in white.

The appearance of the cake seemed to signal time for giving confirmation gifts, because each girl's godparents honored her with a small gift even before hefty slices of cake were cut and served. Emma was pleased to get a length of yellow ribbon from her Uncle Heinrich. Some strips of white lace from her Uncle August confirmed her suspicion that her godfathers must have consulted their sister, Mrs. Mayer, about Emma's needs. She was making herself a hat for Easter, and it was to be decorated with yellow ribbon and white lace.

From her father's sister, Emma received an embroidered handkerchief and from Godmother Koch came a lovely brooch to wear at the high necklines of her Victorian-style bodices. A leather-covered hymnal, with her name embossed in the small space for that purpose on its cover, was her mother's gift to her. Ella received the same. The books reminded the girls of the religious significance of the day. And from their father, the girls got something each had longed for, had whispered to one another about, had imagined in the moments of wishful daydreaming—a ring with a colored stone pretending to be a precious gem, clear enough to spew sunlight in several directions. Their first impulse was to show their friends. They took their leave of family with great dignity, only to lose it amongst their squealing girlfriends.

On a Saturday evening just a few weeks later, another equally joyful event brought many of the same young people in the confirmation group together again: the Mayer children were having a play party in their parents' home. The date had been chosen so the full moon could light the way home for the twelve invited guests. Emma and Ella and the boys made sixteen people—just about all the Mayer parlor could hold when stripped bare of its furniture.

Emil Beckmann was among the young men who had been invited to the party. Mrs. Mayer saw him as one of a relatively few good prospects for her oldest daughter. Mr. Mayer agreed. Emil's father had purchased some farming land along the Pedernales— choice acreage for most any kind of farming, especially cotton, the dominant cash crop in the hill country. Emil was living on that land, and it was well known in the community that the land would become his in time. Emma's parents had counseled her about the importance of marrying someone with good land holdings. The Beckmann land was producing good quantities of cotton, and cotton prices were stable. Emma understood that she could do worse than to marry Emil Beckmann.

In February just past, Emma had received a finely cut paper lace card from Emil. It was a lovely valentine. The printed message expressed romantic sentiments and Emma reread it from time to time, gently removing the delicate card from her handkerchief box where she kept it safe from the inquisitive eyes and hands of her sister and brothers. The card was unmarked by a signature or a handwritten comment. Only the envelope bore the sender's name. She saved that too. Emil was the first young man to show interest in Emma as a young woman.

When the card first arrived, Emma talked with her mother about Emil. The conversation reinforced everything Emma had come to understand about her future: she was expected to get married, to be a homemaker, and to become a mother. Emma felt comfortable with that future. She knew that all her experiences and training had prepared her for those roles. But she yearned for more. She yearned for romance. She wanted to feel her pulse quicken when Emil was near. She wanted to believe that his did too. She wanted to think of herself in a beautiful house like the one she had grown up in, with nice china on a well-laid table. She wanted lace curtains on the windows. She wanted a parlor with peacock feathers and a Victorian divan upholstered in a rich brocade. She wanted a bedroom with a dresser that had a large mirror in which she could inspect her appearance every day. She wanted nice clothes and linens and a sewing machine to make them—the best that money could buy. Sewing with it would be a pleasure. She visualized herself as a young married woman doing chores like those she helped her mother do in a pretty house that had gingerbread trim and a porch swing. When she complained to her mother that all Emil Beckmann had to offer her besides land to farm and a well was a small log house, Mrs. Mayer would say, "You will work together to build the house of your dreams. It will come in time."

From her bedroom window, Emma watched Emil arrive on horseback in the afternoon of the play party. She watched him dismount and greet her parents. His blond hair was carefully plastered in place. His suit was dusty from the ride, but his stiff collar gleamed bright white against tanned skin. She watched as he helped her father and brothers carry the parlor furniture out of doors and smiled at the apparent strength that years of farming had given him. Emil's ability to lift her mother's couch almost single-handedly was appealing.

Mrs. Mayer was watching too, but with trepidation, hoping that no harm would come to the couch she had stintingly saved for and had waited so long to purchase. Fortunately, the weather was cool and dry that afternoon—no threat to the pieces of furniture that stood like castaways in the front yard. For the arriving guests, they seemed beacons of household readiness for dancing and singing and generally having a good time.

In the now unfurnished parlor, Ella was given the task of breaking peppermint sticks into lengths of different sizes. She made two separate piles, putting each set into different hats. The girls would select their pieces from one and the boys from the other.

Finding who had the matching piece of candy was something the girls especially enjoyed. If shrewdly done, it gave them a chance to visit with several boys before finding their partners. All the girls had marriage on their minds. When Emma found that her partner was August Beckmann, Emil's younger brother, she hoped that Emil might try to use his senior status in the family to swap candy pieces with August. He didn't. Emma felt a wave of disappointment pass through her. Determined to remain un-daunted, she took her place in a "Skip to My Lou" formation of partners with August while Emil stood opposite a girl from a nearby farm. As if by magic, as one of the boys began pumping the bellows of an accordion, the German conversation instanta-neously transformed itself into an English chorus singing: "Flies in the buttermilk, shoo fly shoo. . . ." And so the dance began. After several dances, when it was time to change partners, Emil and Emma found themselves standing opposite one another. He smiled. She responded in kind with a demure twist of her head. They linked arms and swung round for the next square dance call.

Several hours later, the front yard was brightened by moon-light, aided by some kerosene lanterns that Mr. Mayer had care-fully hung from the branches of nearby trees. Mrs. Mayer was scurrying to and from the kitchen bringing out platters heaped with sausage, loaves of bread she had baked that morning, several different kinds of cheese, and large aromatic cookies with pitchers of lemonade to wash down the tasty snacks. She placed all this food on the long wooden table that the field hands and sometimes the family used for eating regular meals. Tired out by the square dancing and circle games, the young people welcomed the flavorful and generous food. Besides satisfying the feeling of emptiness they had after such vigorous exercise, the food made legitimate some time for friendly conversation between partners. Snacking also offered a chance to plan the games and dances that would come next. By the time everyone started for home, they had played a variety of different games, reciting all the English verses from memory. At midnight, even young feet and limbs ached for rest.

As everyone expected, Emma and Emil continued to be partners at play parties held at the homes of friends and neighbors. They were also partners at dances held in Burg's Hall. Emil had a one-horse buggy that he'd drive from the land that he and his brother were farming only a few miles distant from the Mayer home. Emma always prepared for these times with care. At her mother's prompting, she had made herself two new party dresses—an extravagance of sorts—to wear when Emil came to call. They were based on the same pattern: high neckline, deeply ruffled yoke, a satin sash to define a corset-cinched waist, and a skirt that fluffed out at her feet with the help of a couple of petticoats.

One evening, Emil found Emma in a yellow dress. Its golden color was especially becoming to her dark hair and eyes. Noticeably charmed by her appearance, he treated her with the care one gives a porcelain doll. He helped her into the buggy, offering her a lap robe even though the temperature was not at all chilly. He moved his horse with a slow gait as much to keep the ride smooth as to increase the time alone with this young lady.

There was hubbub at Burg's Hall. Emma enjoyed being with lots of people, talking and laughing about the ordinary events of life in the Texas hills. Everyone seemed interested in the same things. Indeed, everyone did the same things, held the same values. Some might consider that boring. Emma found it comfortable.

A group of young men got together to form a little band of accordion, harmonica, tuba, and drums. They played polkas with vigor, pressing their volume to its limits to remain audible over the din of a hundred dancing feet smacking the wooden floor. After dancing a frenzied polka, Emma was glad she was wearing black shoes and stockings to the dance. The tops of her ankle-high shoes were covered with the dust kicked up by energetic dancers.

Emma and Emil danced and visited with friends until midnight, when everyone walked over to the building beside the hall. There, Emil bought his partner a meal of sausage, potato salad, beans, and homemade bread with steaming cups of coffee—all for twenty-five cents a person. Joining others at a table where the food was served family style, the young couple chatted with friends while enjoying the savory aromas and flavors of Mrs. Burg's cooking. Their friends had regarded them as "a couple" even before Emma and Emil had acknowledged the increasing permanence of their relationship. No one asked but everyone wondered about the date of their wedding.

On the early morning ride home, Emma's head nodded several times; she was feeling a little drowsy from the good food on top of all that dancing. In an effort to keep herself awake, she chattered about the wedding plans of the young people they both knew. Much of the conversation around the table at Burg's had been about forthcoming weddings. Emil interpreted the girl's chatter as a hint. The time had come, he thought, just as he had anticipated.

Emil reined up the horse at the Mayer house but did not jump out of the buggy right away as was his custom. Emma tensed a little. It was about to happen. She knew how she would respond. Emil took a ring out of his pocket—a simple gold band. Holding it somewhat awkwardly in both hands, Emil looked away from Emma into the distance where the bright moonlight marked a path on the road. Simply and without preliminary statements, Emil asked Emma to marry him. Without comment, she agreed. A little nervous, and quite tense, the two young people somehow managed to place the golden band on Emma's left ring finger. Relieved, Emil now jumped down from the buggy, moved to the opposite side, and helped Emma down. He escorted her to the front door of the house her father had built when she was eleven. He said something about work in the morning, then quickly took his leave. Emma watched him walk back to the buggy, jump in, and drive off, all the time wishing that she did not feel so numb. She turned and entered the Mayer house, the home after which she would model her own as Mrs. Emil Beckmann.

four

Trial Marks

N a flea market near Fredericksburg, I came upon a bottle. It caught my attention because its label bore a name I had heard on several occasions when talking with hill country people: Watkins. The first reference had been made by a hill country woman who spoke highly of Watkins vanilla extract: "the best vanilla extract there ever was," she said with the authority of an experienced cook. But this bottle had not contained vanilla extract. The label reads: "Pain-Oleum" and declares the alcohol content to be an astounding 69%. Stains of reddish-brown color are spattered on the inside of the bottle. The label claims the contents to be "an aid in reducing many forms of pains, swellings, and inflammations." *Might Emma have used this product?*

The bottle itself predates screw caps; its mouth and neck are made to accommodate a cork. Directions for the use of Pain-Oleum are printed on the bottle's label in three languages: English, German, and Polish. From my present-day perspective, I found it curious that Spanish was not among them. The company is listed as the J. R. Watkins Medical Co., in Winona, Minnesota, with distribution centers in New York, Houston, Memphis, San Francisco, and Winnipeg. I knew that Winona had been settled by Poles. And, of course, the Texas Hill Country had been settled by German-speaking people. New York and Houston would have had populations of German-speaking people. But German would not have been a popular language in the United States during

World War I. Therefore, I reasoned that this cork-stoppered bottle of Pain-Oleum most likely was of pre-World War I vintage.

The purchase price of Pain-Oleum is listed as one dollar for eleven fluid ounces. *How expensive was that at the time the product was purchased? What kind of medicine was it? What else did the Watkins Company produce and sell?*

On the reverse side of the bottle, block letters show the Watkins name bold and clear. Just above that name, at a point delimiting about one quarter of the bottle's volume, there appears a raised glass line. Across that line letters formed of raised glass spell the words: TRIAL MARK. *What was the purpose of a trial mark?* Maybe it measured the amount of liquid that could be used and the purchase price still refunded if the customer was not satisfied. I gazed at the bottle for a long time, its shape, size, label, and trial mark clearly of another time. I was impressed by the realization that a bottle which Emma would have considered ordinary was quite unusual to me. I wondered about Emma's use of the bottle's contents. *Did she use Watkins products regularly? If so, what were they? How did she get them?* And then my thinking took a new turn. I examined that trial mark and asked: *What trial marks did the young Mrs. Emil Beckmann make during the first year of her life as a farmwife living in a log house in the Texas Hill Country in 1908?*

One of the best ways to get in touch with any historic persona is to try to imagine him or her going about the processes of living. Having placed Emma in time, I tried to make her come alive in my imagination. I created scenarios from the evidence I had collected, striving to be true to every detail. When parts of my image went blank or out-of-focus, I knew what I did not know about. That helped to focus my questions. The gaps in my imaginings actually directed the search for new clues to Emma's story.

Portfolio of Evidence

HORTLY after my curiosity about the Watkins Company was piqued by the bottle with the trial mark, I came across a contemporary catalogue of the company's products. It listed the company's founding date as 1868. When I had an opportunity, I asked members of Emma's community about

Signpost Artifact Three: In the early years of the twentieth century, the Watkins Company marketed medicinal products in bottles with trial marks like this one.

Watkins products. Everyone raved. Watkins products are the best you can get, they told me. The testimonials of the women, in particular, were impressive. They said that their mothers and grandmothers used only Watkins vanilla extract and preferred the medicines and baking goods sold by the Watkins man. Some remembered visits by the Watkins man when they were children. But the residents could tell me little more. And my letters to the Watkins Company went unanswered.

In search of the story of the Watkins man and his products, I went to the local telephone directory for a Watkins Company listing. The contact I made was disappointing. Like other members of the community, the local Watkins dealer couldn't tell me a great deal about the Watkins salesman of the turn of the century. But he referred me to a rich resource: the Watkins Company District Manager, E. E. Schmidt, who happened to live, like me, in San Antonio. And there was a bonus: Mr. Schmidt turned out to be an amateur historian of the Watkins experience. When I met him, he seemed pleased to share the following information:

> The Watkins salesman was a special person in the lives of farm people. He'd visit with them and talk about the things that interested them. That was good business—a personal touch to salesmanship. He'd tell jokes too. Some people really liked the off-color ones. That added a little spice to their day.
>
> Around the turn of the century, the Watkins man brought his products to the people of the Texas Hill Country in a horse-drawn wagon. The enclosed wagon held wooden crates of Watkins products—each bottle or tin was secured in its own partition within the crate. Painted on the sides of the wagon in bold letters was the name: J. R. Watkins Medical Company. You see, Mr. Watkins started his company in Winona, Minnesota with medicines: tonics, liniments, salves, and veterinary supplies.
>
> The Watkins salesman dressed well. He wore a suit and starched white shirt. In the cities, he even wore a derby hat.
>
> The Watkins man carried free samples with him.

In its early days, the Watkins Company made chewing gum that wasn't for sale. The Watkins man would carry sticks of the gum for children of the families he visited. That was a real treat for those farm boys and girls. He'd also carry samples of Watkins products for housewives and farmers to try. Watkins baking goods were popular among the women, especially Watkins vanilla extract. The men liked the liniments and salves. They'd doctor their children and their animals with Petro-carbon Salve—it was used as a drawing agent and a lubricant for deep wounds, whether inflicted by farm machinery, glass, or barbed wire. Farmers would swear by the miracle-like qualities of Watkins Petro-carbon Salve. Most people had faith in the curative powers of Watkins medicines—like Pain-Oleum, for instance.

Besides baking goods like extracts, flavorings, and spices, the Watkins man brought cosmetics into the farmwife's home. Frequently, the farm woman would feel embarrassed to ask questions about cosmetics for sale in the general store or a drug store in the town where she might shop from time to time. But the Watkins man was a trusted friend. She felt comfortable in the privacy of her home asking him questions about face creams, face powders, colognes, and perfumes. And the Watkins man was happy not only to tell her how to use the products but also to give her a free sample or two. Farm women of the Texas Hill Country discovered beauty products through their Watkins salesman.

Other items in the Watkins line included sewing machine oil, washing compound, louse killer, and polish for stoves and wood finishes.

In the early days of this century, there was only one Watkins man for all of Gillespie County. He'd make his rounds from community to community with his horse-drawn Watkins Wagon. Knowing that he was far from home most of the time, some people would feed him and even put him up at night. Everyone gave him coffee. They'd boil water in graniteware pots, then add freshly ground coffee beans in ample supply to make a dark, rich brew. Some used to add a half-cup of cold water to the pot to help make the grounds settle. Others used an eggshell for the same purpose. Even so, the first cup that was poured always had its share of coffee grounds. No one gave the Watkins man that first cup. He got the best his customers could give. Yes, the Watkins man was a special visitor, a trusted friend.

Mr. Schmidt's comments about the Watkins salesman and his products assured me that Emma had used Watkins products, that she quite likely had been visited by the Watkins man in her home, and that she might have emptied many Watkins Company bottles beyond their trial marks. As an aside, I thought it interesting that my fascination with trial marks was apparently shared by many others: Mr. Schmidt showed me brand new bottles of Watkins vanilla extract for sale to contemporary customers. Once again, they bear the trial mark.

Still curious about Pain-Oleum because it was a medicine whose name sounds quackishly strange to me, I consulted a Watkins almanac in Mr. Schmidt's possession; the company had published it in an earlier era for distribution to customers. Although it showed no copyright date, one of its pages bears a claim that the Watkins Company "has been a 'stand-by' in Farm and City homes" for over half a century. Since the company was established in 1868, this almanac must be a document of the 1920s. And, I noted, by that time the company was simply the Watkins Company, not the Watkins Medical Company, as it is called on the Pain-Oleum bottle—another piece of evidence for the bottle's age.

Although the almanac was obviously not of Emma's young adulthood, I thought that it might refer to Pain-Oleum. I was right. A bottle of the medicine is pictured—cork-stoppered even in the 1920s—and reference is made to its use as a topical treatment for bruises; it was a type of rub. It would take some digging to establish without question the year that the bottle of Pain-Oleum in my possession was made and sold. But all the evidence I had gathered suggested that Emma may very well have used Pain-Oleum to soothe bruises she and Emil sustained when doing housework or farm work. She probably used medicinal and cleaning agents in the Watkins line as she went about her daily chores. I had an idea of what those might have been, but being a city dweller myself, I couldn't clearly picture Emma in my mind's eye doing those chores. That both frustrated and intrigued me. Satisfied that I had learned enough about Watkins products to understand their role in Emma's life, I addressed my inquiry to her work: *What were Emma's jobs as a farmwife in the first decade of the twentieth century? How did she do them?*

Once again, I turned to my "Dr. Watson," my mainstay and touchstone in this search for Emma's story, Ophelia Nielsen Weinheimer. Ophelia could tell me about women's work on Texas Hill Country farms from the perspectives of at least two generations: her own and that of her mother and mother-in-law, the women who had taught her.

In response to my questions about the jobs of farm women in the Albert-Stonewall-Fredericksburg area in the early 1900s, Ophelia wrote out this list:

Milking
Making butter and cheese
Separating cream from milk
Canning and butchering
Making sauerkraut and salt pickles
Putting dried sausage in lard
Taking care of the chickens
Cleaning the hen house
Putting clean straw in nests
Setting hens and marking eggs to be hatched
Making soap
Cooking—baking bread
Washing clothes
Mending
Darning socks
Starching clothes; using cooked starch and raw starch
Ironing clothes
Sewing cotton sacks
Mending cotton sacks
Sewing wagon covers

Sewing clothes for the family
Making quilts (carding cotton)
Making feather pillows and feather beds using chicken
    feathers or duck down
Growing plants for the garden in the hotbed
Tending flower garden and potted plants
Picking cotton
Selling eggs and milk to farm workers
Helping take care of farm animals; giving animals feed
Preparing cane for molasses
Cutting corn tops
Raking hay
Bathing children
Washing hair (using rainwater from cistern)
Getting clothes ready for Sunday
Cleaning lamp chimneys
Trimming wicks and filling lamps with coal oil
Polishing stove
Packing school lunches
Packing Sunday lunch for after church
Shelling corn
Polishing shoes
Teaching children to do jobs while father is in field
Helping another family who had an illness or a new
    baby
Preparing girls for menstruation (making sanitary belts
    and napkins)
Teaching girls to do handwork
Washing children's feet at night (children went barefoot)
Cooking for the threshing crew
Helping children with homework (in English)
Helping children with memory work for school classes

The list is impressive. Putting myself in Emma's shoes, I was
overwhelmed by the many chores and by all that I did not know
about Emma's daily life. I scanned the list for a focus: *What would
Emma have done in a typical week while still a young bride?* I imagined Emma moving about her log house, its swept yard, and the
farm doing some of the chores Ophelia had listed. But the image

was still too vague. So I gave it a specific time. The week of January 26, 1908, seemed like an interesting one to reconstruct partly because Emma was still a bride making "trial marks" at that time and especially because her birthday was just around the corner. On Saturday, February 1, 1908, Emma turned twenty.

I went back to Ophelia with better, clearer questions: *What might Emma have been doing during the last week of January in 1908, just a little more than a month after her wedding?*

Ophelia responded without hesitation:

> Every day, in the morning and evening, we'd bring in the milk cow (usually had two or three) and tie her in the pen. We'd let its calf suck for a while, then put a halter rope around the calf and tie it up so we could milk. We'd leave the milk in one nipple for the calf. Before starting to milk, we'd wash off the nipples to make sure they were clean, then milk into a small bucket. When that was full, we'd empty it into a larger bucket where we put the milk from all the milk cows. It all tasted the same; the cows pastured on the same land and unless they ate onionweed or some other harsh-tasting grass, their milk would be sweet. We'd always work the nipples until the udder was really dry to get the last of the milk—the creamiest. Cats on the farm usually showed up at milking time; they like fresh warm creamy milk too. You could squirt a stream of milk from a nipple and they'd stand on their haunches with mouths open to catch it.
>
> We'd separate the cream from the milk the next day. Some farms had a cream separator. Otherwise, you'd have to let the lighter cream rise to the top of the milk. Every other day or so, we'd churn the cream into butter. The cream would keep for several days in the winter; in the summer, you might have to churn every day.
>
> Not a day went by that we didn't set some milk aside to clabber. By letting it stand a day or so, the milk would turn thick and sour. Then we'd pour the clabbered milk into a clean flour sack to let the whey drip

out. That would be the base for *Schmierkaese,* cottage cheese, made by adding some cream, fresh milk, and salt to the curds. About once a week, we'd make cooked cheese. We'd warm the clabber, then we'd strain the whey from the curds, press the curds as dry as possible, then add baking soda and let the mixture stand until it turned a glazed yellow color. To the cheese, we'd add some milk and butter and salt and cook the mixture until the curds dissolved. This *Kochkaese* or cooked cheese was a staple on the farm, served warm with homemade bread.

Monday was washday. All girls were taught how to do the washing by the older women in their families, usually their mothers. Most girls actually did the family laundry before they were married. But doing your own and your husband's wash is different. If Emil had been fussy about his clothing, Emma would have discovered that during her first few washings and ironings.

I asked Ophelia how the laundry was done. She told me:

We used a large black laundry kettle. It was positioned so that its short legs would fit inside pipes that were sunk into the ground. That left enough space beneath it to build a fire.

The pot would be filled with water—rainwater if it was available or water from the well. Rainwater was preferred because rainwater is softer than the water that seeps through the limestone here.

After the pot was filled, a fire would be built beneath it with twigs. Wooden matches were bought from the local general store. As the fire kindled, logs would be added to bring the flames to full strength under the pot. Lye soap that was cut into small pieces was placed in the pot. It dissolved as the water heated.

Washtubs were placed on a wooden bench. We'd usually use two, one for rubbing clothes on a washboard and one for rinsing them. The clothes were always sorted into piles: men's shirts, sheets and pillowcases, cup towels, aprons, overalls, and rags. The idea was to separate the heavily soiled things from the colored and less soiled or more delicate fabrics. The whitest things were washed first.

Water was put into the washtub. Some water was added from the laundry pot to warm the water. The clothes would be rubbed on the washboard with lye soap, then put into the laundry pot and boiled. A stick, like a broomhandle, was used to lift out the clothes so that they could be put into the clear water rinse.

They'd be wrung out by hand, then put in the rinse water. After the first rinsing, fresh rinse water was placed in the tub. Then several ounces of bluing were added. This rinse was used to brighten the white fabrics. The clothes would be wrung out again and hung on the fence or on a wire line with wooden clothespins.

Before men's shirts were dried, their fronts and cuffs would be starched with cooked starch—starch was diluted with water for the desired stiffness. Bonnets and the detachable collars for men's Sunday shirts would be dried first. Then, on Tuesday, ironing day, these would be immersed in raw starch—starch dissolved in water but not cooked.

Raw starch was heavier than cooked starch. It would make the bonnet brim stand out stiff when it was ironed dry. After immersion in raw starch, bonnets and collars and scarfs and doilies would then be wrapped in a dry towel ready for ironing. Other things that were starched and dried before they were ironed would be sprinkled with water, then wrapped in a towel so that they were damp before the iron was applied. Usually, this dampening was done while the sad irons were being heated on the wood-burning stove in the kitchen.

The clothes were ironed on an ironing board. Sometimes that board had no legs at all. My mother used one that she supported on a table and the back of a chair. Two sad irons were used at once—one for ironing while the other was being heated on the stove.

Ironing, mending, and sewing went hand-in-hand. It was usual for the farm woman to keep sewing projects under way, like a blouse or dress for herself, shirts for her husband, and, when the children came along, clothing for them. She would also make things for the home: sheets, pillowcases, doilies, and quilts. Since cotton was the major cash crop of the hill country farms, women would sew cotton sacks—the canvas bags with shoulder straps that family members and field hands would sling over their shoulders and drag along like a train as they picked cotton, filling the sack as they went. My mother says that making those cotton sacks was the hardest sewing of all. The canvas was so thick, it would break your needle sometimes. I think the same was true of the canvas wagon covers that women had to mend from time to time. But those big jobs would not be Emma's for a while. Harvesting time was yet to come, and the couple would have gotten linens and household items as wedding gifts. At this early time in her married life, Emma was probably making clothing for herself, using a pattern of her own making or one she borrowed, and maybe tatting. Her granddaughter, Joann Beckmann Schott, remembers seeing Emma do tatting to make lacy collars for blouses and dresses and edgings for sheets, pillowcases, towels, tablecloths and napkins, and other decorative household items.

Of course, every day there was cooking to do: breakfast, the noon meal, and the evening meal. A girl learned to cook in her mother's kitchen.

(Edna Beckmann Hightower had told me that her mother never used a cookbook. According to Edna, Emma had only one cookbook in her entire life: the one that came with a new kitchen range she and Emil bought for their Victorian-style home when it was built.)

Ophelia continued:

As the week wore on, the typical farmwife in these parts would do chores like cleaning lamp chimneys and polishing the stove and cleaning house in between seasonal activities like starting and tending the hotbed.

I had, of course, heard the hotbed metaphor used many times to describe activity. But I had never heard of a literal hotbed in the making. I asked Ophelia: *How do you start and tend a hotbed?*

She told me:

The hotbed is usually built on the south side of the house where it will stay warm, protected from the north winds in the cold winter months. It's a bed for planting as long as the wall that it borders, enclosed by a six-inch concrete wall and filled with the best soil and heat-generating manure available on the farm. The cover is a wooden frame made of one-by-fours and covered with chicken netting; it is set over the hotbed to keep out animals. In the winter, you can put a quilt over the chicken netting for warmth. You'd section the bed and in each sow your seeds: cabbage, kohlrabi, beets, cauliflower, and tomato. Cucumber, green beans, and potatoes are planted directly in the garden after the weather gets warm. Then there'd be flowering plants like Sweet William, phlox, and geraniums, cockscomb, and larkspur. The bed would have to be tended every day, watered with a sprinkling can and watched. When the plants were large enough and the weather warm enough—usually by March in this country—you'd transplant the seedlings from the hotbed to the garden.

As I thought about Emma's first year as a farmwife, it occurred to me that the "trial marks" that were truly firsts for her would have been things she did for the first time by herself and for her home and immediate family. One would quite likely have been making a hotbed—an important and nurturing activity that was a primary responsibility of the woman of the house. I wondered where Emma would have planted her hotbed, because the log house in which she was living as a bride still has a porch on its south side—the side of the house that Ophelia said was the best for a hotbed. Ophelia suggested:

When Emma was living in the log house, she probably put her hotbed along the south wall of the smoke house.

Adding to what she had already told me about the farmwife's chores, Ophelia offered the following:

There were many jobs women did in the fields too, like chopping and picking cotton when it was ready. A regular out-of-doors and smelly job was tending the hen house. Hens need straw to nest and sheep like to eat the straw right out of the hen house. So it's important to watch and make sure that the hens have enough. Then there are egg snakes who will swallow the eggs whole. If you want eggs for eating, you have to be vigilant. Some people place hollow white glass eggs in the hens' nests to give those egg-swallowing snakes digestive problems. Once they eat a glass egg, the lump in their bellies won't let them slither out of the openings in the coop that they used to get in. When they squeeze through a smaller opening, the glass egg will be smashed and the snake's done for. Those snakes have humps when they swallow chicks too. But the humps go away as the chick is digested.

To get some chicks as well as eggs for eating, you have to set the eggs. You have to mark them with pencil so you'll know to leave them in the nest to be hatched.

One experience Emma certainly would have had during her early married life was taking a trip to Fredericksburg to go shopping. In late January, she might have shopped for seeds to start her hotbed in preparation for spring planting. A new bride wouldn't necessarily have a complete supply of seeds so she'd have to buy some. There were interesting shops in Fredericksburg at the turn of the century and before. My mother remembers that when she was five years old in 1896, her mother took her into the Lungkwitz millinery and dress shop in Fredericksburg. The occasion was the fiftieth anniversary of the founding of Fredericksburg. Emma would have gone to Fredericksburg now and then to buy hat and dress trimmings, fabric, sewing notions, and other items she couldn't make for herself. Although mail order was available to the people in the Albert-Stonewall community, most preferred to go to town and deal with local merchants. For Emil, this was a necessity. From time to time he would need hardware and repair services for farm equipment. And there were many hardware stores and smithies in Fredericksburg from its early days. A trip to town by horse and wagon (if carrying things to sell or repair) or horse and buggy would have been a full day's outing for residents of Stonewall.

By Saturday, it was time again to prepare for Sunday church and social activities. The farmwife made the family clothing ready for church and, of course, baked and cooked to fix a packed lunch that would be eaten with other members of the community on the church grounds after services. Often, Saturday was the day for washing your hair with gentle bought soap in the beautifully soft but, in winter, painfully cold rainwater that collected in barrels set out for that purpose. They'd heat the water before using it. They used an egg rinse to make their hair shine.

A humorous story surfaced when we were exploring the mundane task of doing laundry on the farm. Alma Scharnhorst Nielsen found among her carefully stored treasures a blouse that she had made for herself when she was sixteen. Besides the extensive and beautiful drawing work done by carefully pulling threads from the batiste fabric, the blouse is interesting because of its gaping holes. Mrs. Nielsen remembered that she had washed the blouse and hung it on a line to dry. The line was a wire strung from tree to tree in the yard. When she went to take the blouse in, she found the holes. A cow had chewed right through the fabric. The story amuses her now, although she remembers being mad at the cow when she found that it had ruined her blouse. *Why would the cow chew holes in the blouse?* The fabric itself would not seem appealing to the animal. Perhaps its appeal was in the starch, or maybe the soap that had been used to wash it. I knew from

Ophelia's description of washday on the farm that lye soap was the washing agent. A quick check of the dictionary definition of lye told me that it is made from ashes, and ashes are defined as the residue of metal salts. *Could it have been that the cow that chewed Alma Scharnhorst's blouse was in need of salt? Or, was the cow attracted by the fat in the soap?*

Mrs. Nielsen's anecdote amused me, but I was also impressed that she had chosen to save the blouse with its holes for over eighty years. Mrs. Nielsen obviously values her craftsmanship. Perhaps Emma valued her own as well. That thought caused me to ask about needlework, especially tatting which Emma's granddaughter had mentioned when talking about her grandmother's skills and tastes. Ophelia referred me to her aunt, Ophelia Scharnhorst Neffendorf, for demonstrations of tatting and crocheting—important skills in the handwork tradition of the Texas Hill Country.

I met Aunt Ophelia in her home in Fredericksburg where she graciously demonstrated her craftsmanship in both process and product. She tatted and crocheted and showed me some of her quilting as well. As she deftly moved her shuttle through the intricate knottings that transform thread into lacy lengths, I began to realize how many hours are needed to tat a few inches of edging. And, as Aunt Ophelia pointed out, tatting permits no errors. You can't unknot threads tangled by imprecision. As I watched her fingers move the slender thread around and over itself and literally make it pass through hoop-like loops, I marveled that most women of Emma's time were expected to have these skills and to use them regularly, given the busy schedule of jobs they had on the farm. Emma and her contemporary farm women couldn't rely on mass-produced and ready-made outfits to the same degree possible today. That accounts for the special place of the sewing machine in Emma's wish list. But what accounted for time-consuming decorative handwork? Aunt Ophelia led me to believe that women viewed their work with shuttles, needles, and hooks as opportunities for creative expression. They could beautify and distinguish the things they wore and used by adding touches of handwrought elegance. Indeed, the products of their creativity today are sold for high prices in antique shops across the nation. Aunt Ophelia certainly viewed handwork as a creative art even as

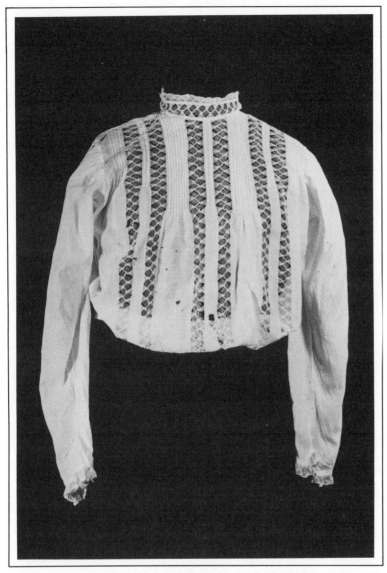

Alma Scharnhorst Nielsen made this blouse when a girl of sixteen. She drew all the thread to make the delicate drawing work herself. A cow ate holes in the blouse while it was drying on a clothesline .

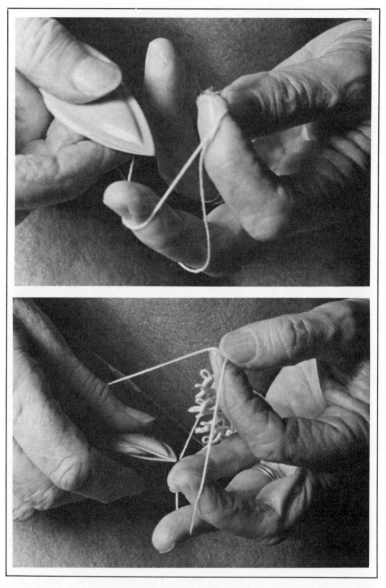

This sequence of photographs shows the manner in which tatting is done. The process is one of knotting thread to create a design that may become a collar for a blouse or dress or an edging for sheets and pillowcases. The last picture in the series shows the difference between edgings that were tatted (left) and crocheted (right) by Ophelia Scharnhorst Neffendorf.

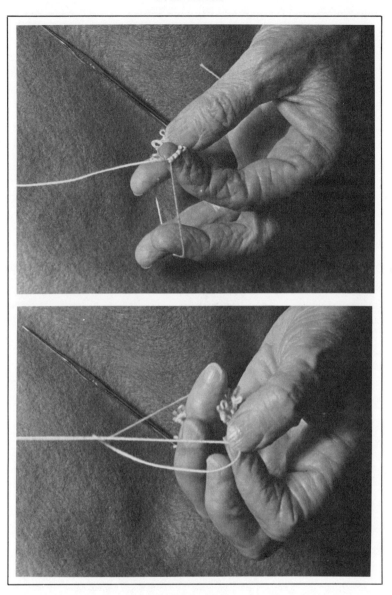

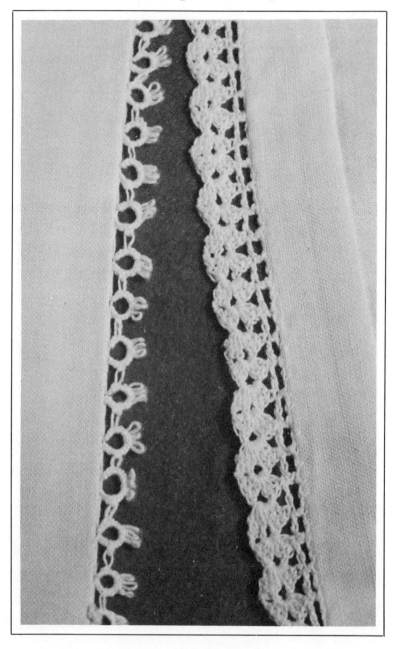

she acknowledged the fussy tediousness of some processes. She commented with pride and some awe about the perfection needed to create a piece of perfect tatting.

When asked about articles of old clothing still in their family's possession, women of the Texas Hill Country sometimes pull from carefully packed boxes and trunks the handworked textiles of their youth, treating them with the respect reserved for artworks. Emma's granddaughter, Joann Beckmann Schott, remembers the high value Emma placed on the arts of handwork and her respect for precision. Emma enjoyed the things she made and the trimmings she fashioned from skeins of thread and yarn as her very own works of art. I cannot help but wonder how many tatting threads Emma tangled and how many stitches she dropped from her crochet hook before she mastered the skills that would later produce her art.

Several hill country women concurred that it was quite likely that Emma would have visited Fredericksburg from time to time, as it was the county seat and the town closest to her Stonewall farm—and still is. Emma might have been motivated to do so during the first few months of her marriage to break up the monotony of daily chores and, perhaps, to reassure herself that the ways of life she knew as a girl in her father's house did not need to be abandoned now that she was a married woman. A shopping trip to Fredericksburg would recall fond memories of town visits that the Mayer family made periodically during Emma's girlhood. It would also carry the promise of self-indulgence that shopping trips hold. For someone like Emma, who had been relatively isolated on a farm, having little contact with anyone other than her husband and family, a shopping trip to Fredericksburg was most likely a source of personal pleasure—in anticipation as well as in actual experience. And what time would have been better than the week before her birthday for the young bride to prevail upon her husband to take her to town? Emma might have gone to Fredericksburg during the week of January 26, 1908, just prior to her twentieth birthday on Saturday, the first of February.

Reconstructing Emma's day in Fredericksburg required information I did not yet have. My questions about how the town might have looked to her and which stores would have been open for her business took me to the office of the local newspaper to find copies of the paper's 1908 issues. I hoped they contained ads for local businesses of the time. The newspaper was a disappointment. What issues there were of *Das Wochenblatt,* the German-language weekly newspaper in Fredericksburg preserved on microfilm, were not well-peppered with ads. And many issues from the year of my interest had been lost.

Then, in the least likely place, I uncovered a gold mine of clues. On the back pages of an old cookbook, after the last page of recipes in the *Fredericksburg Home Kitchen Cook Book,* published by the Public School Auxiliary of Fredericksburg in 1916 are twenty-four pages of advertisements by local businesses. Among the ads of shops for women are those of dress and millinery stores like The Vogue, the Sagebiel Millinery Company, and The Parisian. They offered trimmings and notions as well as hats and ready-to-wear garments. Other stores that might have interested women also appear in the ads: Kolmeier's Hardware, Welgehausen's New York Racket Store (specializing in items priced from 5¢ to 25¢), Hanisch and Payne Drugs, the Oppenheimer Grocery Company, and the R.C. Bonn General Store. But that was in 1916. *Were they doing business in January of 1908?*

I needed a street map of Fredericksburg in 1908, or better yet, 1907. The local Chamber of Commerce didn't have one. Neither did the newspaper. The library didn't have one either. But the National Archives held some clues in the form of fire insurance maps. There are four maps of the town in the set made by the Sanborn Insurance Company. Dated 1895, 1902, 1910, and 1924, those maps contain a wealth of information: building size, location, structure, material, and function as well as the layout of the town. Two maps, the ones for 1902 and 1910, offered a starting place for reconstructing the Fredericksburg Emma would have known in 1908.

My reasoning was that if I compared the 1902 with the 1910 fire maps, I could determine what had changed and what had remained the same in the town over the eight-year period. But when I examined the maps, I was overwhelmed. The town of Fredericksburg was considerably larger and more varied in 1902 than I had imagined. And it had grown substantially by 1910. Fredericksburg at the turn of the century was definitely not a frontier outpost. Indeed, the fire insurance maps for each year were in several parts. Imagination came to my rescue. By visualizing Emma in my mind's eye walking into stores on the streets of Fredericksburg in 1908, I naturally had to ask: *Which ones? In which section of the town should she have spent most of her time shopping?* Those questions narrowed the area of my investigation to the length of three blocks along San Saba Street (presently Main Street) where both maps showed the greatest concentration of shops and stores. As I examined the structures along the length of these three blocks on the 1902 and 1910 maps, I was intrigued by 'the very particular information they held about change and stability in the town. A one-block example illustrates some of the more obvious changes over those eight years:

1. All the windmills present in 1902 were gone by 1910 but the water tanks associated with them remained.
2. Several buildings were added to the section shown in the upper left-hand corner, the block on the southwest side of San Saba, between 1902 and 1910.
3. The saloon and livery stables remained, a barber shop was added, and a photographer's studio was removed. Perhaps it is the same photographer who had a studio on the other side of the street in 1910; perhaps it is not— another direction for research at another time.
4. The functions of some buildings were changed, like the dwelling at position 253 on the 1902 map that had become a general store by 1910.
5. The general store at position 250 on the 1902 map had lost some of its windows by 1910 (so had the bank at position 258).
6. A sign of technological development is the drugstore near the bank which also served as a telephone exchange in 1910; in 1902 that lot was vacant.
7. A tin shop at position 294 was, it appears, about to be replaced by two shops; the 1910 map shows two shops in that location and indicates that the map entry was made *From Plans*. (This turned out to be a clue of considerable importance to my search.)
8. A jewelry store became a cobbler shop (position 291); the nearby barber shop retained its function over those eight years.

9. At some time within that period, the hall and bowling alley were converted into a movie theatre and beer hall.

And there was more. The maps prompted me to ask many questions about the town's development. If I had allowed questions about Fredericksburg's growth to direct my inquiry, I might have lost sight of Emma's story. *How could I determine what the almost twenty-year-old Emma might have seen in Fredericksburg's business district?*

Emma would have seen the buildings along San Saba (Main Street) that appeared on the maps of both 1902 and 1910. So, I drew my own map of Fredericksburg's business district by recording only the structures that appear to have remained the same over those eight years, whether or not they changed in function. I knew that I would be missing some places: those that were present in 1902 and removed after 1908 and those that were built after 1902 and present in 1908. But the task of identifying every possible structure that Emma might have seen in late January of 1908, even over only three blocks, was much greater than I cared to take on. I redirected my search to focus on my original question about a shopper's experiences, attending only to shops or stores she might have visited. Still, there were gaps to be filled.

My principal exhibit—my ace in the hole—was the town itself. Conservation-minded citizens insured that many of the buildings from the turn of the century are still standing. And, although adaptive restorations have preserved only the original appearance of the buildings, allowing them to serve different purposes today from those that Emma would have known, I thought I could trace the gaps in my 1908 street map from information on historic markers, lintels, and cornerstones. I began my self-designed walking tour of Fredericksburg's business district with my own map in hand.

A few buildings boast historical markers that tell their stories over the years of their existence. Those offered little challenge. It was easy to determine whether or not they were present and housing businesses in 1908—their markers said it all.

Information on the Wahrmund Millinery Shop was not easily obtainable in library files but came from an old photograph. In a research library in San Antonio, I found several late-nineteenth-

and early-twentieth-century photographs of buildings in Fredericksburg. Some of the buildings depicted housed businesses when the photograph was made. Several of those buildings still exist. To determine how closely the facades then resembled those today, more than three-quarters of a century later, I compared the old photo with a new one made from the same perspective. One of the photographs showed Mrs. George Wahrmund's Millinery and Dressmaking shop, pictured with several women, girls, and young children in front of the shop and a man and woman (Mr. and Mrs. Wahrmund perhaps?) on the balcony. My first thought was that the shop might have been one that Emma knew. When I found the building, now a savings and loan, in present-day Fredericksburg, I was happily surprised by its authentic restoration. The building looks much as it must have looked to Emma. The historical marker revealed that the shop existed as a millinery and dressmaking business when Emma was a child. But in 1908, although Emma might have seen the building, she would have known it not as a women's dress and hat shop but as a boarding house. *Where would Emma have gone in January of 1908 to find women's apparel?*

Among the advertisements in the *Fredericksburg Home Kitchen Cook Book* of 1916 was one for The Vogue. During the years of her girlhood and young womanhood, Alma Scharnhorst Nielsen had occasion to buy from the Gold sisters, the women who owned and operated the store. From her report, the shop's high fashion merchandise matched its name. Mrs. Nielsen wasn't sure of the site of The Vogue on present-day Main Street. Her daughter, Ophelia Nielsen Weinheimer, remembered it as being on the same block with the Fredericksburg Bank and next door to Welgehausen's New York Racket, also advertised in the 1916 cookbook. *Which buildings on the Sanborn maps did they occupy? Were they in business in 1908?*

Sometimes I found it easy to match the blocks on my map with the limestone and rock buildings along the town's Main Street. Other times, the absence of cornerstones and other identifying marks made the task difficult. In still other cases, the available clues could lead to faulty conclusions.

On the 1902 and 1910 fire insurance maps, the Bank of Fredericksburg appears at position 289. Just down the block from

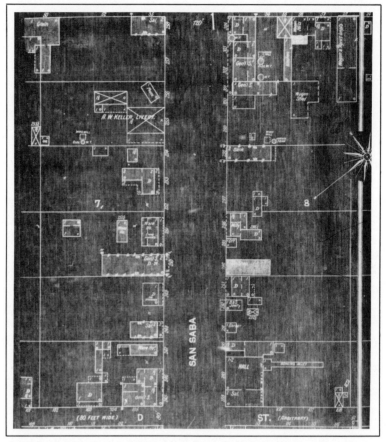

Compare this block in Fredericksburg, from the Public Square to D Street, on the Sanborn Insurance Company's 1902 map with the same block on the fire insurance map of 1910.

the bank, on the 1910 map, is a structure consisting of two units with a stairway between them. It is located about in the middle of the block. A walk to the site placed me directly in front of *der Kleider Schrank,* a clothing store for large women. A step inside the store brought me face to face with the present shop owner, whose family has resided in the town for several generations. She verified that her shop is in the same building that once housed The Vogue. She told me that the shop had carried ready-to-wear ladies' clothing and millinery. Women could also have apparel made to order. The Gold sisters were, it seems, seamstresses of

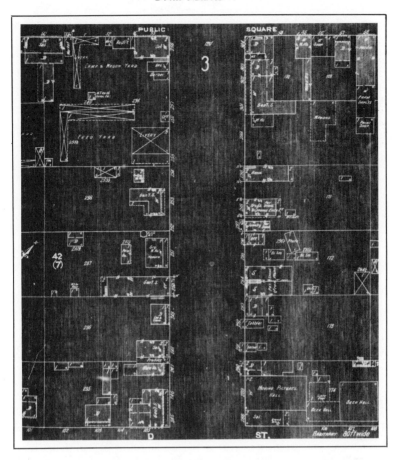

some refinement and skill. They also sold laces, ribbons, and other trimmings and notions for making clothing and decorating hats. As I stood there listening to the present shop owner reminiscing about The Vogue's reputation as voguish, I imagined Emma entering the shop and stopping to admire the latest fashions hanging on metal clothesracks that once ran the full length of the shop's wall. Emma probably purchased fabric, sewing notions, and trimmings in The Vogue. She may have gone there every time she got to Fredericksburg, if only to look at the latest styles to get ideas for her own sewing. Then she could stop next

This street map of Fredericksburg's business district is drawn from the 1902 and 1910 fire insurance maps of the town made by the Sanborn Insurance Company. Buildings shown along San Saba (present day Main Street) are those that appear on the fire insurance maps for *both* years. Blackened areas identify those places that appear to have been serving the same purposes in 1902 and 1910, as noted in the key. Outlined structures are those with changed functions over the years; the key indicates those changes. *Which businesses might Emma have visited on a shopping trip to Fredericksburg just prior to her twentieth birthday?*

Key Functions of Numbered Structures

1902	1910		1902	1910
1. Saloon	Saloon	28. Bank	Bank
2. Livery	Livery	29. Dwelling	Dwelling
3. Dwelling	General Store	30. Jewelry	Cobbler
4. Warehouse	Warehouse	31. Barber	Barber
5. General Store	General Store	32. Dwelling	Dwelling
6. Dwelling	Dwelling	33. Hall	Movie Hall
7. Saloon	Saloon	34. Saloon	Saloon
8. Warehouse	Warehouse	35. Dwelling	Warehouse
9. General Store	General Store	36. General Store	General Store
10. Dwelling	Dwelling	37. Vacant	Vacant
11. Hardware	Hardware	38. Dwelling	Racket Store
12. Dwelling	Dwelling	39. Store	Store
13. Restaurant	Store	40. Jewelry	Dwelling
14. Dwelling	Saloon	41. Saloon	Saloon
15. Dwelling	Restaurant	42. Dwelling	Dwelling
16. Drug Store	Saloon	43. Harness Shop	Saloon
17. Dwelling	Dwelling	44. Dwelling	Dwelling
18. Dwelling	Dwelling	45. Millinery	Millinery
19. Dwelling	Dwelling	46. Insurance office	General Store
20. Grocery	Hardware	47. Dwelling	Tin Shop
21. Coffin	Coffin	48. Dwelling	Dwelling
22. Dwelling	Dwelling	49. Dwelling	Dwelling
23. Dwelling	Dwelling	50. Dwelling	Dwelling
24. Dry Goods	Dry Goods	51. General Store	General Store
25. Blacksmith	Dwelling	52. General Store	Dwelling
26. Dwelling	Dwelling	53. Nimitz Hotel	Nimitz Hotel
27. General Store	General Store		

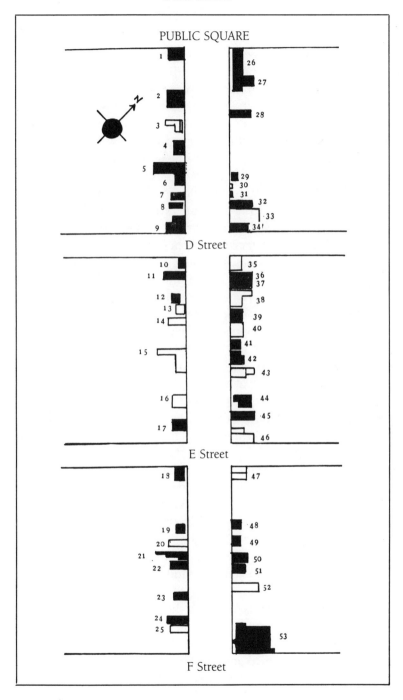

PUBLIC SQUARE

D Street

E Street

F Street

door for small but indispensable items like hairpins, combs, and thread.

But why hadn't I recorded the shop on the map I drew from the 1902 and 1910 Sanborn maps? I went back to my original sources of information. There on the 1910 fire insurance map appear the buildings I had found just down the block from the Bank of Fredericksburg. They weren't on the 1902 map, which would account for why I hadn't recorded them on my hand-drawn map, but that didn't mean that The Vogue and The New York Racket were not in operation in 1908. A more careful re-examination of the 1910 map helped me to find the evidence to correct my imagination. Within the outlines of the structures that became the shops in question a parenthetical notation reads (*From Plans*). *Why? Did that mean that the buildings had not been built yet in 1910?* It seemed so; I couldn't be sure. And researching the two businesses in question would have been an extensive project in itself. I decided to remove The Vogue and The New York Racket from my imaginary shopping list for Emma's 1908 visit to town. I was content to think that she might have shopped in them in 1916 (but there were other things going on in her life then).

Alma Scharnhorst Nielsen remembers going into Louisa Lungkwitz's shop with her mother when she was only five years old. The time was May 1896, the fiftieth anniversary of Fredericksburg's founding and a cause for the town's celebration. She remembers her mother buying a new hat for the occasion in that shop. According to Mrs. Nielsen, the building in which Mrs. Lungkwitz had her millinery shop hasn't changed much over time. It appears as a millinery shop on the fire insurance maps of 1902 and 1910. Quite likely Emma knew it as such.

Several general stores appear on the map; their buildings are still standing in the town. The same can be said for hardware stores and saloons and dwellings. Emma must have walked by several and shopped in some now and then when she and Emil spent a day in town.

If, on one of her trips to Fredericksburg as a young woman of nineteen or twenty, Emma had looked toward the southeast end of San Saba, she would have seen the ship-like structure known as the Nimitz Hotel, owned and operated by the grandfather of the child who stands in front of the hotel in the 1891 photo. The hotel

Mrs. George Wahrmund's millinery and dressmaking shop in Fredericksburg. This photograph was probably made in the 1880s or 1890s by the Kilman Studio in Fredericksburg, Texas.

has been restored by the Texas State Department of Parks and Wildlife and is now a museum. Even today, it is a distinctive, striking building; it differs dramatically in style and material from other buildings in the town. Emma certainly couldn't miss seeing it as she and Emil rode into town from Stonewall and as they made their way homeward. To Emma, the people who stayed at that hotel and the grandson of its owner, just a couple of years older than herself, lived in a world very different from hers even though they walked along the same streets of a town in Central Texas. The boy in the photo was born in 1885; he would become the distinguished Admiral Chester A. Nimitz, Commander-in-Chief of the U.S. Naval Fleet in the Pacific during World War II. Admiral Nimitz was from the area; Emma was of it. He made his contributions to the town of his birth, the nation, and the world. Emma made hers too. By living the entirety of her life in the Texas Hill Country, Emma Mayer Beckmann helped to preserve the rural German-American culture of her homeland.

Emma's Story

ONDAY, *January 27, 1908*
A blustery late-January wind whipped the corners of the Beckmanns' log house. Emma appreciated the warmth given off by the thick logs of dried oak burning in the kitchen stove. The fire Emil had helped her build earlier that morning cooked the sausage and eggs for breakfast and heated the small kitchen. Despite her inclination to stay in the pleasant warmth generated by that small stove—the item she had valued less than other home furnishings in her dowry—Emma braced herself for the outdoor chill and her resentment of a recurring chore: doing the wash.

It couldn't be put off another week. There were too many overalls and shirts and sheets and towels to clean, not to mention the menstrual rags of the past week. After all, she didn't have many things left that were clean, and it wasn't raining. Fortunately, her mother had given her a supply of lye soap so Emma didn't have to try her hand at making it alone yet. This bride was

According to Mrs. Nielsen, the building in which Mrs. Louisa Lungkwitz had her millinery shop hasn't changed much over time. It appears as a millinery shop on the fire insurance maps of 1902 and 1910.

The Nimitz Hotel in 1891. The future Admiral Nimitz is the boy standing in front of the structure that bears his name. *Photograph made by the Kilman Studio of Fredericksburg, Texas.*

discovering how different it was to do household chores without a loving mother's watchful direction.

Though the early morning air was chilly, a winter sun directed its diffused rays onto the place just beyond the area of the front yard where Emma would start her laundry fire. She probably was grateful for her knitted undershirt and the bulky wool sweater she pulled over her high-necked heavy cotton blouse. Her petticoats and the drawers underneath them added weight to her long woolen skirt. A bonnet encased most of her hair—some dark wisps at several places on her forehead and at her temples softened the overstarched look of the bonnet's hard brim. These clothes and the exertion of moving pots, building a fire, carrying pails of water, and rubbing clothes on the washboard would bring Emma close to perspiring on this chilly Monday in January.

Actually, Emma found the cool moist air refreshing as she walked out the door of the well-heated kitchen. The afterscent of fried sausage permeated the log room. On a full stomach, it was no longer pleasing. The starch she had cooked with the heat of the breakfast fire was now cooling atop the small stove.

Emma grabbed the handle of the big iron kettle she used for laundry and, with effort, hauled it to the spot where Emil had sunk three lengths of iron pipe into the ground. She placed the pot's stubby legs into these tubular stands, securing it at a height just right for building a fire underneath.

Water had collected in the barrel Emil had set out to catch the winter rains from the gutter along the edge of the roof. Emma scooped this precious liquid into the laundry pot until it was three-fourths full. In the space directly under the pot's belly, she started a fire with some dry twigs and the wooden matches she kept in a metal match holder fastened to the kitchen wall. When the flame was full and strong, she added logs to make a steady glowing heat. Emma cut the pie-shaped wedge of lye soap into small pieces and put them into the warming water. As the temperature of the water increased to a rolling boil, the pieces of soap dissolved, making a milky-looking brew with an aroma that promised to bleach even the dirtiest of clothes.

The heat of the fire and the exertion made Emma's face redden. She wiped her brow, took off the sweater, and rolled up her long sleeves in preparation for work in the washtubs.

She set up two on a wooden bench and filled one with water from the rain barrel—water scooped out with a pail and carried the several steps from barrel to washtub. Into the second tub, she put well water for rinsing. By the time she had filled the second, Emma could feel the soreness growing in her arms and back. But she went on, next sorting the clothes into piles: Emil's white shirts, sheets and pillowcases, cup towels and aprons, colored fabrics, then heavily soiled things like overalls and rags. She filled a bucket with some of the bubbling soapy water in the black wash pot. Then by pouring it into the cold water in the washtub, Emma made a warm bath for the clothes she washed first, rubbing each in turn with the caustic lye soap on the ridged washboard. Taking each pile in turn, she worked from the least soiled to the most soiled things. She rubbed them, then boiled them in the kettle, then, lifting them out of the bubbling cauldron with a long stick, she placed them in a tub of rinse water. White things got one more dunking in a second tub of rinse water to which she had added several ounces of bluing to brighten all the white clothes.

Before hanging Emil's white shirts by wooden clothespins on a wire clothesline, Emma immersed their cuffs and fronts in the pasty starch she had made earlier that morning. This would make them stand stiff and straight when she ironed them on Tuesday. The detachable collars would be starched with raw starch. Wringing the bulky bed sheets that felt as if they were weighted down by gallons and gallons of water was heavy work. The veins stood out on the backs of her hands with each gripping and twisting motion. Emma stopped a moment to rest.

The really difficult laundry was the last to be done—all those soiled towels that did heavy duty in the kitchen and those menstrual rags that would be carefully cleaned and saved for the next menses. She had soaked them in lukewarm soapy water for what seemed like an eternity, and while rubbing them with the lye soap on the washboard, Emma reminded herself to buy a bottle of Cardui the next chance she had. The bottle of medicine that relieved her cramps was just about empty now.

By this time, Emma's arms and back were throbbing. She pressed the palms of her hands against the small of her back, then arched it to relieve some of the tension she felt there. The good feeling it produced was suddenly intensified by a familiar and welcome sound—the plodding of horses working in tandem to turn the creaking wheels of the Watkins Wagon. The coming of the Watkins man meant a welcome relief from this dreadful laundry. She knew that the tubs would have to be emptied, the laundry things put away for another week, and the drying clothes gathered, folded and sorted in readiness for Tuesday's ironing. But all that could wait for a bit. The Watkins man was here.

Like the people of her community, Emma saw the Watkins salesman as a trusted friend. He had been bringing Watkins products to her family home for as long as Emma could remember. Everyone valued those products as the very best in baking goods, medicines, stock supplies, and cosmetics. Emma recalled how her mother always gave the Watkins man a meal when he arrived. Mrs. Mayer used to say that the Watkins man had to travel a far distance from the comforts of home to bring his products to her door. He deserves consideration, she'd say while setting another place at the Mayer table. Emma also remembered how she and her sister and brothers waited for the Watkins man to give each a stick of Watkins chewing gum. That would satisfy them, and they'd run off to play while their mother examined the Watkins products to make her selections. Now Emma would be making the selections. Suddenly she felt very grown up.

The Watkins man bounded out of his wagon looking dapper in his white shirt with starched collar and cuffs and a suit like the ones Stonewall farmers wore on Sunday. Emma's mother had always appreciated the Watkins man's tidy appearance. Having just finished the hard work of laundering clothes, Emma too could appreciate the touch of refinement his appearance added to her surroundings. She also liked the respite from chores that his visit made legitimate.

Emma invited the Watkins man into her kitchen. As he set his sample tray on the table, they chatted a bit about the weather and about what was happening on neighboring farms he had visited in the past few days. Emma filled the graniteware coffeepot with water and placed it on the stove to boil. The stew she had made earlier simmered on the back of the stove. Emma knew the Watkins man would stay for lunch. She made the invitation. He accepted. They got down to business.

The sturdy wooden Watkins tray had partitions just large

enough to accommodate sample sizes for the varied products of the J. R. Watkins Medical Company. There were liniments, tonics, salves, ointments, tablets, lotions, and powders for human ailments and for veterinary purposes too. Emma was most interested in the baking goods. With her birthday at the end of the week, she was thinking of baking a cake and cookies in celebration of turning twenty. A large bottle of vanilla extract was a must. The Watkins man reminded Emma about the trial mark on the bottle, but she assured him that she had already tried Watkins vanilla extract many times over. No need even to think about getting a refund for the unused portion. All of the contents of the bottle would get used in a hurry, she assured him. Emma asked for a can of nutmeg and one of cinnamon and some black pepper. The Watkins man let her sniff the aromas from his sample tins. It was a ritual Emma remembered seeing her mother practice. Now she was the one making the decisions about what to buy. It felt good.

When the Watkins man went out to his wagon where wooden cases held a seemingly limitless supply of products, Emma put healthy measures of coffee into the pot of boiling water. She let it boil a few minutes, then removed the pot from the stove and added an eggshell to help the coffee grounds settle. By the time the Watkins man had returned to the kitchen, she had poured two cups of steaming dark coffee. He carried into the room the baking products that Emma had selected and some samples that he would give her in anticipation of her birthday, samples of products that held fascination for the young woman: cosmetics. One by one, he introduced Emma to the Watkins line of beauty products.

He showed her a jar of face cream and told her how to use it in addition to her sunbonnet to protect her skin from the bright rays of the Texas sun. And he gave her a free sample.

He showed her face powder that would help her achieve the illusion of a porcelain-like complexion for special occasions. And he gave her a free sample. She asked how to apply it and he showed her. Emma went to look at herself in the mirror that hung over the washstand where Emil shaved outside the kitchen door. She was pleased by the flawless appearance the powder gave her skin.

He let her sniff the scents from bottles of fragrant toilet water and perfumes. And he gave her a free sample of the one she liked best.

He showed her some sweet-smelling liquid shampoo and eight different kinds of toilet soaps. Emma couldn't resist. She ordered a bottle of shampoo and a bar of soap that smelled like rose petals. She would use them for special occasions.

On his trip to the wagon to complete Emma's order, the Watkins man crossed paths with Emil, who was coming to the house for lunch. From her place in the doorway, Emma could see Emil's quizzical look at the products the Watkins man held. She called to her husband, "They're for my birthday." Emil scowled.

The diplomatic Watkins man handed Emil a free sample of Petro-carbon Salve. That placated Emil a bit. Some discussion of veterinary aids followed, continuing as the two men walked into the kitchen and seated themselves at the table. It continued as Emma served deep bowls of beef stew thick with swollen beans, and as they dunked large chunks of buttered bread into the hearty gravy.

The visit from the Watkins man had made Emma hungry for talk. There had always been someone to talk to in her father's house. Sometimes she felt marooned on her husband's farm. That evening, she prevailed upon Emil to take a trip to Fredericksburg during the week. He was reluctant. Emma reminded him that the coming Saturday was her birthday. Couldn't they go to town so she could buy a new hat? An extravagance, Emil said. Emma negotiated: to buy new trimmings for an old hat? Then she reminded him of the hardware he'd been saying he needed to repair the wagon. He conceded.

On Wednesday, January 29, Emma was up at five. Before they could go to Fredericksburg, she had to do the milking, feed the chickens, and make sure the hen house was in order. She also had to prepare and serve breakfast, do the dishes afterwards, and pack her bag for an overnight stay at a friend's house in town. The short winter days made that mandatory if they wanted enough time in town to make the most of the five-hour trip by horse and buggy. Emil had chores to do that morning too. Even so, they were on the road to Fredericksburg by eight.

It was midday by the time they passed the Nimitz Hotel on the wide and dusty main street called San Saba. A light drizzle helped to keep the dust on the road, though the buggy wheels churned enough up to spot Emma's duster. She pulled the duster closer around her dress in a protective motion. As she did so, she took notice of several women and men who were chatting in front of the Nimitz. The women were wearing the latest in fashion. Their velvet hats caught Emma's notice; the brims curved up, away from the large pompadours atop their heads. The crowns were piled high with feathers and bows. Emma couldn't take her eyes off them. Even as the buggy was almost to the coffin shop on the left side of the street, Emma was twisted around, gawking at those hats. Emil chided her for appearing ill-mannered. She turned forward, sulking a little over the reprimand.

They proceeded on down San Saba, past dwellings decorated by pretty wooden gingerbread trims and tin siding that Emma wished for her own house. They passed Mr. and Mrs. Clark's boarding house with its large doors and gingerbread-trimmed balcony.

Emil reined up the horse in front of a simple building of well-placed stone blocks. Its plain flagstone porch was covered by a pitched roof, held up by simple slender columns of wood. Emma was delighted to discover that she was just a few yards from that hat she wanted even more now since she had seen the stylishly dressed women at the Nimitz. She turned and smiled at Emil. It was sweet of him, she thought, to bring her right to the place. In his usual manner, he said little more than that she should meet him later at the restaurant across the street. He was going to the hardware store and smithy. He'd pick up the coal oil and lamp wicks they needed. She was free to shop for herself. Emma knew that this was Emil's birthday gift to her. She smiled, helped herself down from the buggy, and stood facing the Lung-kwitz millinery shop, savoring the pleasant anticipation of buying something new for herself.

Emma lifted her skirts to step up onto the flagstone porch. Through the glass-paned double doors to this combination home and shop, Emma could see the promise. She entered and was greeted by the scent of potpourri. Colorful ribbons hung draped over a table near the center of the front room where Louisa

Lungkwitz ran her business. On other tables were untrimmed hats, bolts of cloth, feathers, lengths of laces in different widths and patterns, and silk flowers. The familiar rhythmic sound of a treadle under the foot of a skilled seamstress told Emma that Mrs. Lungkwitz was at her sewing machine, probably filling someone's order for a custom-made garment. Louisa Lungkwitz realized Emma's presence and emerged from the next room to greet her customer cordially.

The conversation literally poured from Emma at the sight of the other woman. Shopping trips were always important opportunities to visit with people you didn't get to see very often—to catch up on what was happening beyond the borders of your own farm. Being a good businesswoman, Mrs. Lungkwitz understood this and accommodated her customers. She listened, nodded, smiled, and added a little local gossip now and then until Emma had spent her craving for contact with another woman. Then they got down to business.

Aided by Mrs. Lungkwitz's knowledge of fashion trends, Emma selected an untrimmed hat of deep brown velvet, some ostrich feathers, and lengths of a lighter brown and burnt orange velvet ribbon to make into decorative bows. Those colors would compliment a brown dress she had made for herself just before her wedding, the one she trimmed with a white tatted collar. Emma looked at the makings of her new hat, visualizing how she would appear in it at Sunday church services. The vision pleased her. And she asked Mrs. Lungkwitz to charge the several dollars the hat and trimmings cost to an account Emil would pay off when their crops were sold.

Emma was delighted with her purchase. She had to contain her enthusiasm and hold back from bounding through the door swinging the satchel she had brought to town to serve as a shopping bag. She reminded herself that she was almost twenty. She took her leave of Mrs. Lungkwitz in a dignified manner and proceeded out the shop's door, turning right toward the general store on the next block.

Emma found several acquaintances in the general store and enjoyed another opportunity for friendly conversation and some gossip before she selected the seeds for her hotbed. She chose some kohlrabi, beets, cabbage, and cauliflower seeds and several types of flowers. And she decided to buy another type—one she hadn't discussed with Emil. She had often admired the pots of impatiens that her mother kept on her porch. In fact, they were Emma's favorite flower, perhaps because she associated them with her mother and joyful times of family gatherings on the front porch. What better way to give the front porch of her log house some color and to make it feel more like home, she thought, than to place some potted impatiens here and there. So she indulged herself and bought a few seeds of the flower: white, red, and pink. It's only a few cents, she reasoned. She had sold enough eggs to cover the bill.

It was still early in the afternoon when Emma had finished her buying and talking in the general store. She took time to walk along the streets of this town she'd known since she was old enough to accompany her parents on their shopping trips. The sun was shining now. This late January day in the Texas Hill Country would match the warmth Emma felt within herself. She knew this place like the back of her hand. She could look at a building and remember what it had been when she was a child. She could look at vacant lots and predict—with a little help from town gossip—what would be there next year. She passed the White Elephant Saloon and knew who was likely to be there. She passed the rock and limestone homes with their distinctive gingerbread trims and knew who lived within them. She was very much a part of this town. Emma wondered what lay in store for her in this place where she felt so at home.

Thursday, January 30, 1908

Their horse pulled the buggy southeast, past the Nimitz Hotel and out of town at daybreak. It was another chilly damp morning. Emma was glad to have the lap robe she tucked around her legs and feet. Her cotton bonnet was quilted to protect ears and hair from cold breezes as well as the hot sun. She had enjoyed the respite from farm tasks that the trip had allowed and, especially, the chance to talk with people she knew but saw only now and then. Emma liked people; she really didn't care for the isolation of the farm.

A typical winter Texas day, she thought, while throwing back the lap robe that had become too warm by the time Emil directed the horse through the gates of their farm's pastureland. It'll be a good day for making the hotbed, she cautiously suggested. Emil agreed without his usual arguments about all the things he had to do. Emma was pleased.

It had taken until late morning to get home. Several chores had to be done and lunch had to be made before either of them could think about a hotbed. They unpacked the buggy: Emma gingerly carried the makings of her hat into the house and set them on the table near her sewing machine, where they would remain undisturbed until she could attend to them. Emil brought the coal oil and lamp wicks into the house and a new kitchen pot he had gotten at the hardware store. He left Emma to tend to the milking and lunch while he unhitched the horse. Near the farm wagon that would be needed at cotton-picking time, he dropped the hardware he had bought to make needed repairs.

In early afternoon, Emil readied the place on the south side of the smokehouse where he had poured a cement wall for Emma's hotbed. The frame cover waited only for the chicken mesh he had bought in town. Emil mixed some of the best soil on the farm— some he collected from near the Pedernales River—with cow dung and filled the cement enclosure. Now Emma could sow.

Emma enjoyed the feel of the good soil between her fingers. Leaning over the concrete wall, she made even sections by drawing furrows with a small stick. With the same stick, she made little shallow holes in the soil; she didn't try to make them equidistant, just far enough apart so the seedlings wouldn't be crowded. The kohlrabi came first. The next section was for beets, next for cauliflower. She continued with the vegetables in no particular order, just the way she pulled the little packages from the pocket of her apron where she had put them when she unpacked her shopping satchel. But she would remember the sequence even if no one else could see any pattern to her sowing. The vegetables were most important to sow, and she dropped them into the soil first. She saved a place in the hotbed for some flowers, but before sowing the phlox, Sweet William, and geranium seeds, she scooped some of the rich soil mixture into three old pots. These would be homes for the impatiens.

Before she had finished, Emma's back muscles were complaining. She was too pleased with her handiwork to care. A couple of daylight hours were all she had left now. Quickly, she took the new watering can Emil had bought for her in town to the rainwater barrels and scooped out as much of the precious liquid as the can would hold. The seeds in the hotbed got a good dousing. Later Emil would place the cover over them and, in motherly fashion, Emma would tuck them in for the night with a quilt fastened on top of the chicken mesh—a quilt she had saved for just that purpose.

By the time she had done the supper dishes, Emma was too tired to start anything else, even though she was aching to trim her hat. No sense, she thought. To begin by the light of a lamp after so tiring a day would run the risk of ruining ribbons or feathers.

Mr. and Mrs. Emil Beckmann retired earlier than usual that night. It had been a good day—and a long one.

Friday, January 31, 1908

Emma rushed about to finish her routine tasks: milking, sweeping the yard, checking the hen house for snake intruders, setting the eggs she needed to have hatched, then separating the cream from the milk. Today, she'd have to make cheese; two days had passed without making cottage cheese or cooked cheese. She wanted to make butter too. She needed plenty. She was going to bake a cake and two kinds of cookies for her birthday. And she had to find time to trim her hat. With relatives certain to come by for long afternoon visits on Saturday, there would be no time to have the hat done by Sunday unless it was done today.

When Emil came into the kitchen for lunch, he savored the sweet spicy smells of baking cookies—large ones boasting cinnamon and sugar and Watkins vanilla extract. Their marvelous aroma and the welcome warmth of the kitchen triggered pleasant, loving memories. He tugged playfully at his wife's apron strings and when she turned to scold him, Emil kissed her on the mouth. There was nothing more. He sat at the table and Emma served him lunch. But the warm kitchen was warmer for the unspoken exchange.

Finally, well into the afternoon, Emma had baked all that she was going to bake, had cleaned all that she planned to clean, and had supper under way to the point where it needed no help from her, only a long steady heat from the stove's burning logs. Emma carefully washed her hands in the basin outside the kitchen door, dried them thoroughly, then sat down at the table where the brown velvet hat, velvet ribbons, and fluffy ostrich feathers had been waiting for her touch since she had put them there a day ago. She fingered them gently and not without some trepidation. Velvet was not forgiving. Ostrich feathers did not rebound from too much handling. She knew that there would be no replacing them in the near future. Emma was about to make a trial mark that the whole community would see. She wanted it to be good.

Sunday, February 2, 1908

The congregation of Trinity Lutheran noticed approvingly when Mrs. Emil Beckmann arrived with her husband to attend church services. She wore a brown shirtwaist dress and velvet hat to match. The girls and young women admired the billowing bows, the colors of rich earth and summer sunsets. The older women took note of two ostrich feathers, jauntily angled along the edge of the brim, as if readied for flight. Emma Mayer Beckmann was a proper twenty-year-old matron of her place and time. She felt the approval of her neighbors. And she savored the good moment.

Cotton Bolls and Gingerbread

T was, after all, the house—that lovely Victorian-style house—that had led me to Emma in the first place. It was the house that had justified my enthusiasm for Emma's story when I was asked, *Why Emma Mayer Beckmann? Why not someone else, someone less ordinary?* The reason was because her house still stands and I had access to it. I had come to enjoy that house not only because it had been Emma's but because it is of a particular place and time, and it represents a way of life that belongs to people I had come to know in the Texas Hill Country as I searched for Emma's story—a life history very unlike my own.

I had waited to explore the story of the Victorian-style farmhouse until after I had learned something about the woman who made it her home. It was easier to make sense of the information I collected if I tried to maintain some sense of the chronology in Emma's life. That was sometimes more difficult than I had thought. Only in books and other materials designed to present and instruct does historical information come in neatly organized, clearly sequenced components of human experience. Typically, it "hangs around" in bits and pieces, sometimes hidden in old drawers, cabinets, and minds, and usually scrambled together with odds and ends.

I often found myself making folders to contain information I had gathered incidentally, from artifacts and testimonials, about interesting historical facts that seemed to have little bearing on my search for Emma's story. Sometimes, what I discovered was quite pertinent to Emma but referred to a time in her life that came later—after the time I was trying to reconstruct at the moment. Early in my search, the Victorian-style house was less relevant as I tried to identify Emma herself. But now I was ready to study it.

The house not only had a commanding presence, but it was physically there for me to enter, to walk through, to look at, to sense, and to experience every time I visited the place where Emma had spent her entire adult life. It was quite natural that I approached its study with considerable emotion when my inquiry into Emma's story permitted me to return to the place where I had first met my historic persona.

The charm of the house derives from its cottage-like simplicity. It has only three rooms of almost equal size, about thirteen by fifteen feet. Two are separated from the third by an indoor hallway (referred to as a *durchgang* among German residents of the area) that extends from the decorative front door, off the front porch, to a rear door opening onto a smaller back porch. A gingerbread pattern decorates front and back porches. The kitchen is separated from the house by an outdoor hallway (another *durchgang*); it is located beside the stone building that was present when Emma moved to the farm as a bride. *What does the layout of the house tell about the family's lifestyle?*

I had been told by several people that the Victorian-style house had probably been built around 1915. *Was that the correct date?* Henry Beckmann, the son of Emil's brother, Otto, remembered that his father had lived in a stone structure next to the log house. That building became Emma's kitchen when Otto left, after Emil bought Otto's share of the land. *How could Emma and Emil afford to buy more land and build a new house too? How much did the land and the house cost? How was payment made: on credit or in cash?*

Emma and Emil's resources certainly must have been related to farming. During the time they were farming, cotton was the cash crop of the hill country. When I talked with Mr. and Mrs. Schuch about their childhood in the area, they spoke of growing up in cotton fields. Edna Beckmann Hightower did too. The people at the state park said that the barn was built in the same year as the house. And the Beckmanns added a frame section to the stone building at that time too. That would have been an ex-

Signpost Artifact Four: Emma moved into this Victorian-style house from the log house several years after she and Emil were married.

pensive investment for the still-young couple. *Was cotton bringing good prices in those days? What was influencing the cotton market?*

The house had sparked many questions. What intrigued me most was the suspicion that the Victorian farmhouse connected Emma and Emil with the larger world, seemingly far removed from their immediate environment.

Portfolio of Evidence

walked through the pasture and the gate to the right of the tank house, past the outdoor hallway that connects the stone building, with its frame addition, to the Victorian-style house, and stepped onto the front porch.

The front porch with its gingerbread trim reminded me of many I had seen in the Texas Hill Country. Its resemblance to the house in which Emma had grown up is unmistakable (the Mayer house is pictured on page 31). Emma's house is surrounded by a swept yard: a dirt yard that serves as a firebreak between the grassy pastureland and the building. The space underneath the porch is covered by latticework to keep out small animals. There is no cellar or basement; the absence is testimony to the difficulty of digging into the limestone-based terrain. A porch swing suggests that this extension of the house into the out-of-doors was a place for socializing and relaxing on a Sunday afternoon or a summer evening. I was struck by the contrast with houses in city suburbs: today socializing and relaxing occurs in the backyard, not on the front porch. Few suburban houses have front porches, and when they do, their function is decorative. Sitting in front of most contemporary houses would be a public activity. Emma's front porch overlooked the farm; the next-door neighbors were acres away.

Emma had a back porch too, but it is substantially smaller than the front one. Its size suggests that it served more as a passageway from the back door to the backyard than as a place to sit and talk. It too was trimmed with gingerbread, in a pattern pleasing to contemplate. Its intricate cutout design was different from any others I had seen among the hundreds of examples on houses in Fredericksburg and sections of San Antonio.

I was also intrigued by the pressed tin covering on the outside walls of the house. It gives the appearance of stone blocks like those used to construct the Mayer house. Pressed tin seems to have been an economical way of making a frame house look like it was built of the more expensive stone blocks. Of course, everyone knew it was covered with pressed tin; that was stylish. The pressed tin work also marks Emma's house as a product of the Industrial Revolution, when an illusion of heavy stone blocks could be manufactured in a lightweight house covering.

Just a few feet from the back porch, outside the fenced area, is the hen house, an important source of egg money for Emma but a smelly place even when well-tended. I think that Emma would have wanted access to the backyard via the back porch but probably didn't sit on that stoop-like structure for rest and recreation very often.

The smokehouse where the smoke from live oak bark was used to flavor bacon, ham, sausage, head cheese, blood sausage, and liver sausage is behind the house. In the sand that covers its floor, Emma might have stored sweet potatoes for winter use. At the rear of the smokehouse there used to be a ladder leading to the loft where Edna Beckmann Hightower told me she and her younger brother, Elgin, played when they were children. The only other entrance to the smokehouse is the front door that leads directly to the area where the food was stored. That front door can be entered directly from the backyard; the front wall of the smokehouse interrupts and is part of the fence surrounding the yard.

That is also true of the tank house in the front yard. Its front wall interrupts and is part of the yard fence. Both structures were present when Emma and Emil moved onto the farm. The Victorian-style house with its fenced yard came later. It seems that the fence was built with the distinct purpose of insuring easy access from the house and yard to the places where food and water, respectively, were stored. So the front of each building became part of the fence; no gate hindered Emma's movement in and out of those places. Access to both buildings was possible but not easy from any direction except from within the yard itself. There

The front porch of the Victorian-style house is shown in the photograph on the left. The back porch appears in the photo to the right. Note the differences and similarities between the two structures.

The hen house situated to the rear of the house and outside the fenced swept yard.

is only one door on each and it faces inside the yard. Perhaps that was a form of security. It certainly was convenient for Emma, who probably spent most of her time in the area defined by the fence's perimeter.

The tank house is also interesting because the tank is fed water by a windmill. It reinforces that Emma's life had been greatly affected by the Industrial Revolution. Without the windmill to pump water from deep beneath the limestone rock and without the technology to drill beneath that rock, Emma would have had to rely on whatever water a hand-dug well could produce and on water carried from the Pedernales River. The windmill and storage tank kept her supplied with considerably more water than she could have had otherwise. But even though the machine was there to help, it didn't release her from nature's forces: a good breeze was needed to pump the water from the ground. Emma's life was influenced in seemingly equal degrees by nature and technology. By contrast, technological forces in the latter part of this same century have a decided edge over the natural ones that affect our daily lives.

Shutters on the tank house suggest the presence of windows. Here Emma had a small work area with ready access to water that

The smokehouse to the rear of the Victorian house. It has only one main entrance: the door that appears in this photograph. A ladder at the rear of the building permitted access to the loft.

flowed from the cyprus tank down to a small faucet at the front of the building. By opening the shutters, Emma could permit air to flow through the small stone room. Here she could hang things to dry protected from the elements—even onions—and this was probably where Emma kept the things she used for washing.

The front door of the Victorian-style house is decorated by beveled glass, and just inside is the hallway where I first saw Emma and Emil's wedding portrait and pictures of their children. The placement of the inside hallway in relation to the other rooms and doorways suggests that the family seldom used the main door off the front porch. There were too many other places to enter the house. The inside hallway was most likely the place for receiving guests. From the center of the inside hallway, one can look straight through one doorway to another that leads to the outside hallway, and almost directly across that space is another door leading to the kitchen in the older stone building.

All doorways have transoms—a missing structure in most residences built in more recent times. The placement of doors and windows in the house was probably intended to promote cross-ventilation in warm weather and to conserve heat in cold weather by allowing each room to be closed off from the others. The house has neither air conditioning nor central heating.

To verify my hunch that the doors and windows had been placed to conserve heat and to promote air circulation throughout the house, I made a freehand drawing of the house's floor plan, using actual measurements of each room. That sketch did more than verify the air-flow patterns in the house; it gave me some idea of the family's living patterns and priorities. For instance, the children's room was within earshot of the places where Emma probably spent most of her time: the kitchen, the outside hallway, and the yard where smokehouse, hen house, and tank house are located.

There are seven doorways in all. The children's room can be closed off from the neighboring master bedroom, which has its own door opening onto the front porch. Another doorway can close off the children's room from the inside hallway, which has doors on either end, one leading to the front porch and one leading to the back porch. The children's room was obviously shared by all. Most of the family traffic probably moved back and forth

The tank house elevates the cyprus tank to permit the gravity flow of water. Like the smokehouse, the tank house is entered from inside the yard. Also like the smokehouse, its front wall interrupts and is an extension of the fence around the yard.

If you stand in the center of the indoor hallway, just inside the front of the Victorian house, you can see the outside hallway through symmetrically aligned doorways.

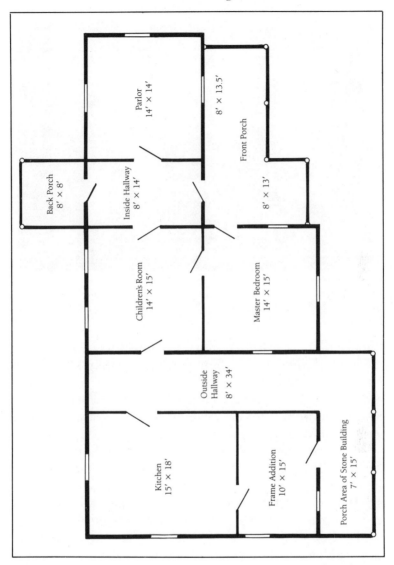

Parlor
14' × 14'

8' × 13.5'

Front Porch

Back Porch
8' × 8'

Inside Hallway
8' × 14'

8' × 13'

Children's Room
14' × 15'

Master Bedroom
14' × 15'

Outside
Hallway
8' × 34'

Kitchen
15' × 18'

Frame Addition
10' × 15'

Porch Area of Stone Building
7' × 15'

This floor plan of Emma's house offers some clues to the Beckmann family's lifestyle.

The all-purpose or children's room in the Victorian-style house is entered from the outside hallway. The doorway to the left of the dresser leads to the master bedroom.

through the outside hallway into the children's room and through the master bedroom to the front porch. Apparently, security was not an issue for Emma and Emil. The house layout boasts ease of accessibility. But there is one place set apart. You have to cross the inside hallway to enter the room reserved for special occasions and for formal entertaining: the parlor.

The parlor intrigued me more than any of the other rooms because, though it is roughly the same size as the others, it differs from them in the absence of a doorway leading directly to the outside, making it "off the beaten path." Other things also caught my eye. The pine floor is not covered by area linoleum like the floors of the other two rooms and the kitchen. Those who reconstructed the furnishings of the house for the period of about 1915 to 1918 placed a woolen area rug on the floor just as Emma might have done. If linoleum floor covering was used to sustain heavy traffic, its absence in the parlor underscores the probability that the room was not used as frequently as the others. As in the master bedroom, striped paper rather than paint finishes the walls, and there is evidence of much more woodwork than is typical in contemporary houses. In both the bedroom and the parlor, dark

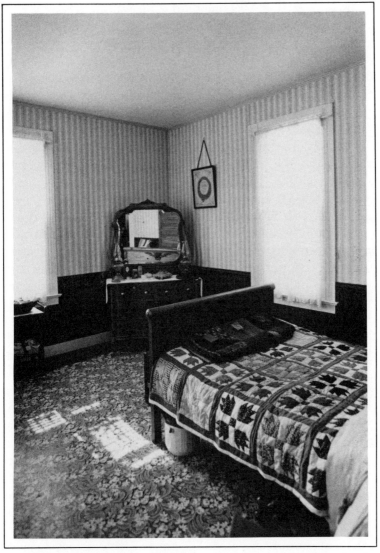

A view of the master bedroom. The doorway to the front porch is located to the left, outside the frame of this photograph.

wainscoting rises up over one-third of the wall all the way around the room. The walls in the inside hallway are covered with ceiling wood (beaded wood) from floor to ceiling. Woodwork is everywhere evident in all the rooms: frames around doors, molding along the upper edge of the walls, and baseboards where wall meets floor. Obviously, a great deal of skilled carpentry was required to build this house, and that would have affected its cost. While the house is not grand, it is nicely finished inside and out.

In the corner of the parlor is a wood-burning heater. Flues to accommodate a heater are evident in every room of the house. It would be possible, then, to heat each room independently and to close off those not in use to contain needed heat in the living quarters; it was unlikely that all rooms were heated every day in the winter. The kitchen would have been the center of family living, especially in the wintertime when cooking kept it warm and gave it appetizing aromas. The parlor was probably kept closed and unheated most of the time. Even in the summer, the room was probably kept closed when not in use because opening the windows would permit dust to enter; ventilation of air through the remaining rooms can be accomplished easily by opening all doors and windows in the master bedroom and the children's room.

Although none of the present furniture was Emma's, I was struck by the dominant presence of the couch. Emma had listed a "sofa" in addition to the "living room suite" in her wish list (Signpost Artifact Two). The couch is certainly intended for the more genteel aspects of living.

Across the outside hallway from the house is the stone structure where Otto Beckmann lived while Emma and Emil were living in the log house. A washstand just outside the screen door that leads to the kitchen indicates the absence of running water in the house. Inside the house is a massive wood-burning range, like one Emma would have used. The range, which has a commanding presence, was manufactured by the Charter Oak Stove and Range Company in St. Louis—a major distribution center when the railroad was the prime mover of freight in this country. I had visions of Emil taking the wagon to the station in Fredericksburg to pick up the new range (a much better stove than Emma had recorded in her wish list), one they had ordered to outfit the room in which Emma would spend most of her time cooking for and

The top view of the parlor shows the doorway leading to the inside hallway. The bottom view shows the Victorian-style couch against the front window.

The screen door of the stone structure leads into the kitchen. A large range commands one wall. A long wooden table stretches almost the length of the room. These reconstructions present the room as it was most likely maintained by Emma.

feeding her family. The room also contains a table which probably is like the one Emma noted in her wish list. It would have provided work space as well as an eating area. Other smaller tables increase the work area. Emma's daily cooking may have required more space than most people require today. There was much mixing and rolling out to do. Without running water and refrigeration, she no doubt found food preparation and preservation time-consuming. Emma probably spent much of her day in the kitchen, a place where informal visits with friends and relatives took place, probably over food at almost any time of day.

The more I thought about the importance of the kitchen in Emma's life, the stronger was my assumption that she would not have moved out of her log house kitchen until she could move into the kitchen in the stone building. That "newer" kitchen could not have been developed until Otto had left the premises. It seems that the Victorian-style house was most likely built soon after he left.

At this point in my detective work, I realized more than I had before how important dates are for forging connections among events. A rude realization detoured my thoughts: the railroad did not reach Fredericksburg until 1913. If my imagined scenario of Emil picking up the new range at the Fredericksburg station was plausible, it had to have happened no earlier than 1913. I assumed 1915 to be a reasonable year for the new house. But I still had no clear-cut evidence.

Several pieces of information that had emerged from my earlier conversation with Edna Beckmann Hightower now seemed relevant to my search for the story of the house. Edna had told me:

> My Mama and Daddy moved into the log house when they were married. There was the log house and the rock house. When I was a little girl, they built the wood house. We had to watch that Elgin didn't get hurt. He liked to crawl along the *durchgang*.

The baptismal records at Trinity Lutheran Church showed three children born to Emil and Emma Beckmann: Reuben, Edna, and Elgin. Edna's birth year was 1910. Elgin, the youngest Beckmann child, was born in 1914. In 1915, Edna would have been five and Elgin a toddler capable of crawling in dangerous places.

This kitchen in the log house was the one in which Emma did her cooking until the Victorian-style house was built and the kitchen moved to the stone building.

Perhaps the house was built in 1915. The growing family would need a larger and more substantial house than the log and stone buildings already on the land when Emma moved there. But the family's economic condition would also have had something to do with the time selected to build a house.

No one in the community was sure of the exact year that the Beckmanns built the frame house. Even the published report of the archaeological study completed by the Texas Department of Parks and Wildlife before reconstructing the Sauer-Beckmann Living History Farmstead does not contain much information about the Victorian-style house. Perhaps, I thought, fire insurance records held a clue. I called Stonewall Farm Mutual and asked: *Do you have a record of insurance for the Beckmann frame house? And, if so, do the insurance papers give an appraised valuation of the house?* Unfortunately, the answer was a courteous no. The old records had been lost. Where could I turn now? Maybe the county tax assesser/collector's office would have a record of house appraisals for school tax purposes.

Records of property taxes paid by Emil Beckmann from 1908 through the next decade showed no increase to suggest that a house had been built on the property. The county clerk who assisted me in finding those records assured me that the property was assessed for both the value of the land and the structures built on it, but the records gave no hint of when the new house might have been built. What they did show was that Emil had increased his land holdings in 1916: the number of acres on which he paid taxes increased in that year. That verified some information I had been given by Edna Beckmann Hightower, that her father had bought adjoining farm land from his brother, Otto. *How much did that land cost? If the Victorian-style house was built at the same time, how were Emma and Emil able to afford so many big expenditures?*

I knew, of course, that making an accurate assessment of Emma and Emil Beckmann's resources and debts was probably not possible. Many papers would have been lost and some things might never have been written down. But I could get some idea about the status of their land ownership by examining the deed records at the county courthouse. If I could find out whether and when they had debts on their land, I would have some idea of the family's economic situation. The other important piece of information would come from investigating their cash crop: cotton.

In the deed and release records that specify transactions in Emil Beckmann's name (predictably, there was none for Emma), four contain useful information. Only two are reproduced here to serve as examples; they seem to be the most important keys to assessing Emil and Emma's resources. The contents of the other documents are summarized in the interpretation that follows.

One release reads:

Hermann Beckmann,   to   Emil Beckmann.
> The State of Texas.
> County of Gillespie. Whereas by deed dated the 15th. day of May, A.D. 1908, recorded in the deed records of Gillespie County, Texas, Vol. 17 on pages 192–193 and 194, Hermann Beckmann conveyed unto Emil Beckmann, all that certain tract or parcel of land lying and being situated in the County of Gillespie, State of Texas, known and described as follows:—Two hundred five and 4/5 (205 4/5) acres of Sur. No. 5 originally granted to Maria J. Guerrero, said 205 4/5 acres fully

Trinity Lutheran Church Records
Stonewall, Texas

	Name	Birthdate	Baptismal Date	Parents	Sponsors
p. 39 # 78	Reuben Adolf August	6 Nov. 1908	24 Jan. 1909	Emil & Emma Beckmann	Adolf Gerhard August Duer* Olga Beckmann Ella Mayer
p. 43 # 112	Edna Emma Wilhelmine	26 July 1910	14 Nov. 1910	Emil & Emma Beckmann	Emma Baag Wilhelmine Wilke Carl Tatsch Edgar Mayer
p. 49 # 186	Elgin Walter Hugo	3 Sept. 1914	8 Nov. 1914	Emil & Emma Beckmann	Hermine Petsch Hedwig Wilke Walter Baag Hugo Mayer

These baptismal entries appear in the records of Trinity Lutheran Church.
*The spelling of this name was unclear in the handwritten entry.

described by metes and bounds in above referred to deed which is made part hereof; And whereas as part consideration for said land and premises, the said Emil Beckmann executed his promissory note of even date with said deed in the sum of Twelve Hundred dollars, payable to the order of Hermann Beckmann at Fredericksburg, Texas, on or before six years after its date, bearing interest at the rate of five per cent per annum from May 15th, 1911, and providing conditionally for the usual ten per cent attorney fees and a vendor's lien was retained in said conveyance to secure the payment thereof; And whereas the said Emil Beckmann has paid the said note and all interest thereon unto me, Hermann Beckmann, legal owner and holder of said note; Now, Therefore, Know all Men by these Presents: That I, Hermann Beckmann of the County of Gillespie, State of Texas, for and in consideration of the premises and the full and final payment of said note, both principal and interest, the receipt of which is hereby acknowledged, have remised, released, quit claim, discharge and acquit unto the said Emil Beckmann his heirs and assigns, the vendor's lien heretofore existing upon the land and premises herein and in said deed described. Witness my hand this the 31st day of January, A.D. 1917.

Witnesses:
Henry A. Meier
Hermann Beckmann
H. Meier Sr.

The record of Emil's purchase of land from his brother Otto reads:

Otto Beckmann   to   Emil Beckmann
The State of Texas
County of Gillespie   Know All Men By These Presents, that I, Otto Beckmann, of the County of Gillespie, State of Texas, for and in consideration of the sum of Ten Thousand ($10,000.00) Dollars to me paid and secured to be paid by Emil Beckmann of the County of Gillespie, State of Texas, as follows; The sum of Two Thou-

sand Fifty ($2050.00) Dollars cash in hand paid, the re-
ceipt of which is hereby acknowledged and confessed
and Seventy Nine Hundred Fifty Dollars ($7950.00)
evidenced by two promissory notes of even date here-
with, the first in the sum of Nineteen Hundred Fifty
($1950.00) Dollars, due December 1st, 1916, bearing
interest at the rate of seven per cent per annum, after
maturity, and one note for the sum of Six Thousand
($6000.00) Dollars due on or before five years after
date and bearing interest at the rate of seven percent per
annum after December 1st, 1916, cash respectively, and
payable to the order of Otto Beckmann at the law office
of Martin and Martin, at Fredericksburg, Texas, interest
due and payable annually, and providing for ten per
cent additional on the amount of principal and interest
then due as attorney's fees, if placed in the hands of an
attorney for collection, or in case suit is brought on
same, and failure to pay said note or either of them or
any installment of interest when due, shall at option of
the holder, mature each and all of said notes. Have
Granted, Said and Conveyed, and by these presents do
grant, sell and convey, unto the said Emil Beckmann, of
the County of Gillespie, State of Texas, all that certain
tract or parcel of land, being 205 acres and being 93
acres out of Survey No. 7, Maria Juanita Trevino and
112 acres of Survey No. 5, M. J. Guerrero and bounded
as follows: Beginning at a stake 117 vrs. South of Pedernales River and in West line of tract conveyed to
Hermann Beckmann by F. Sauer and wife by deed dated
the 20th day of December 1900, recorded in Gillespie
County Deed Records in Vol 7, pages 610–612: Thence
South with said west line 1010 varas, stake for S.W. corner of this tract being N.W. corner of a 12 varas strip
sold by F. Sauer to G. Bauer by deed dated February 14,
1900 recorded in Gillespie County Deed Records in
Vol. 7 pages 268–270; Thence east 114 vrs. with North
line of said 12 vrs. strip to stake for S.E. corner of this
tract; Thence north 1010 vrs. stake in east line of said
land conveyed to Hermann Beckmann by F. Sauer and

wife; Thence West 1147 vrs. to the place of beginning. The land herein conveyed being the same tract of land conveyed by Hermann Beckmann to Otto Beckmann on May 15th, A.D. 1908 and Recorded on the 9th day of June A.D. 1908 in Deed Records of Gillespie County in Vol. 13 on page 634. To have and to hold the above described premises, together with all and singular the rights and appurtenances thereto in anywise belonging unto the said Emil Beckmann, his heirs and assigns forever; and we do hereby bind ourselves, our heirs, executors and administrators to warrant and forever defend all and singular the said premises unto the said Emil Beckmann, his heirs and assigns against every person whomsoever lawfully claiming, or to claim the same, or any part thereof. But it is expressly agreed and stipulated that the vendor's lien is retained against the above described property, premises and improvements until the above described notes and all interest thereon, are fully paid according to their fact and tenor, effect and reading, when this deed shall become absolute. Witness my hand at Fredericksburg, Texas this 17th day of February, A.D. 1916.

($2.50 documentary stamp   Otto Beckmann
attached and cancelled)

According to the above deed records and additional ones on file in the Gillespie County Courthouse, the story of the Emil Beckmanns' land acquisition and indebtedness has these parts:

1. On February 17, 1916, Emil paid his brother Otto $2050 in cash and indebted himself for $7950 to purchase from Otto the 205 acres of farmland that adjoined the 205 4/5 acres he had obtained from his father, Hermann, soon after he married Emma.
2. On December 6, 1916, Emil paid off a promissory note for $1950 against the cost of the land he had purchased from his brother Otto.
3. On January 31, 1917, Emil paid off his debt of $1200 to his father for the land on which he and Emma had been living since 1907.

4. On August 26, 1920, Emil paid off the rest of his debt to his brother for the land: $6,000.

So it seems that Emma and Emil were doing well enough in early 1916 to pay, in cash, $2050 for land. And by the end of 1916 and at the beginning of 1917 they were able to pay off two land debts for a total of $3,150. Within one year's time, they paid out $5200. I wondered: *What did it cost Emma and Emil to live? How much did they make by farming?*

My earlier inquiries into Emma's work as a farmwife had made me aware of the high degree to which she and her family lived off their own land. The farm produced much of the family's dairy foods and produce. Emma milked her own cows, raised her own chickens, gathered and even sold eggs, and raised her own fruits and vegetables (which she canned for use during the winters). She needed to purchase very little besides flour, coffee, sugar, and some condiments (possibly bought from the Watkins salesman); she even kept her own yeast cakes. *But what about meat?* She could can fruits and vegetables for use in the nonharvesting times of the year, but without refrigeration, meat wouldn't stay fresh for very long—especially in summer. If Emil butchered a calf, most of the meat would spoil before Emma could prepare it for her family's food. If they had to buy meat during the hot-weather months, their cost of living would skyrocket because Central Texas enjoys considerable warmth from May through October. Then I learned about the butcher clubs from Charles Weinheimer, who remembered helping his father distribute some meat when he was a child.

He remembered that the Beckmanns belonged to the same butcher club as his father. Usually about sixteen families in an area would organize a club. They'd decide when to start butchering, how much a calf should weigh, where and when the quarters of beef should be distributed, and where each member should pick up his meat. The members drew numbers to determine when to butcher. If a farmer drew a number that required him to slaughter a calf first and he didn't have a calf that was heavy enough, he might swap numbers with another member of the club so that his turn would come later.

The calves selected for slaughtering weighed 250 to 300 pounds dressed. At the end of the season, farmers who had slaughtered lighter calves reimbursed those who had contributed heavier calves. There was never much money involved in this settlement because around 1915 calves sold for seven or eight dollars per head.

Another decision made at meetings of the club was to whose house the quarters should be delivered to be cut into the desired cuts of meat and who should receive the front quarter or hind quarter. Then for the rest of the summer, they alternated the quarters. Each farmer came in the evening, bringing with him a pan and a clean cloth for covering the meat. The butchering and meat-cutting was done on Monday so that the families would have meat for the week.

Charles was with his father, Hugo, when the elder Weinheimer delivered a quarter of meat to the Beckmann farm. Emil had a special place on the porch of the old house where the meat was hung and weighed. Mr. Beckmann would put a meat sack around it to keep the flies away. That evening, the men of four families would cut up the meat to share it. If women came along, they'd socialize until the work was done. They'd carry their portion of meat home in a pan covered with a clean cup towel.

The butcher clubs continued until electricity came to the Stonewall area in the 1940s and made refrigeration possible for many people.

I asked Mr. Weinheimer about how much it had cost to live on a farm in Stonewall or Albert around 1915. He told me:

> Most farm families in the area could live on thirty to seventy dollars per year. The only things they couldn't raise for themselves would be flour, sugar, and coffee. And large quantities of those commodities could be purchased at relatively small cost: one dollar would buy twenty pounds of sugar. They'd raise their own food (vegetables, meat, and fruit) and feed for their stock. The rest of their acreage (about half of the typical two-hundred-acre farm) was used to grow cotton.

So, it seems that Emma and Emil needed little cash to keep themselves and their children well fed all year long. Incidental expenses for necessities and small luxuries probably required only small expenditures of cash in the course of a year. Emil paid out

$5200 between 1916 and 1917. If it cost the family even several hundred dollars to live in a year, their total cost for that one year would have been about $5500. *What about the cost of a new house and barn?*

I could find no information on the Beckmann house in the county's records. I called the local lumber company that had been in business at the turn of the century, but the firm's early records were no longer available. I called the company that had restored the house when the living history farm was developed, but they had found no records of the house's origins. I went back to the county courthouse in the hope that some document in one of the files would hold a clue to the house's date and cost. Nothing! Then one of the clerks suggested that if Emil had built the house on credit, there would be reference to that transaction in the *Mechanics Lien Record*. I felt a surge of renewed enthusiasm, an enthusiasm that had flagged from frustration. But I found no reference to Emil Beckmann in the index. As I scanned the listings of agreements that involved some financial credit in the years from 1914 to 1918, there was no mention of Emil Beckmann or Emma's Victorian-style house. I almost put the handwritten bulky ledger back into its storage place in the county clerk's office when a new thought occurred to me. Maybe there was no direct reference to the Beckmann house in any official record. Emil may have paid cash for the new house (that too was an interesting thought). I knew that the kitchen was placed in the stone building in which Otto had been living. It seemed likely that Otto would have left the premises when he sold his land to Emil. That was in 1916. *Might that have been the year when the Victorian-style house was built?*

Here again was a question for which I could find no precise answer. The best I could do was make a reasonable estimate based on the information I had. The house was probably not built before 1914 because Edna remembered her little brother crawling around the place where the house was being built; he was born in 1914. I'm inclined to think that Emma and Emil would not have begun to build until they had purchased Otto's share of the land; that was in February 1916. But there was the possibility that informal agreements between the two brothers had made it appropriate to begin building in 1915, before official transactions were drawn up and registered in the county's deed records. Or, might they have waited until 1917? More often than not, I discovered the chronology of life stories is imprecise. In trying to determine the year of the house's origin beyond any doubt, I developed a new respect for the term "circa."

Assuming that the house was built sometime between 1915 and 1917, I still didn't know how much it had cost Emma and Emil. I wasn't likely to find a receipt. But I could look at records of other people's transactions with the F. Stein and Son Company—the major building company in the Fredericksburg area at the time. Those lien records tell the type of house contracted for and the cost. From them, I could infer the approximate cost of the Beckmann house. These examples are excerpted from the records:

1915 Alfred Frantzen and Wife to Franz Stein and Son
"L" frame and shingle roof dwelling, 28' × 28' × 12' to be built in Fredericksburg. Cost: $200.

1916 Ad. Deckert to F. Stein
Two story frame house, 16' × 32', 18' high with two story porch and shingle roof to be built in Fredericksburg. Cost $655.

1916 Walter Pettit and Wife to F. Stein and Son
Building materials and assistance in building the house. Cost: $618.81.

1916 Wm. Feller to F. Stein
One story frame building 38' × 28' with one gallery 34' × 8' containing three rooms 14' × 14' and two rooms 12' × 14' and one hall 10' × 14', shingle roof, gallery roof covered with tin, rooms and hall to be ceiled, three rooms wallpapered, inside woodwork painted and stained. Cost: $1075.

1918 Christian Fritz and wife to F. Stein and Son.
All lumber building materials and supplies, except tin for roof, necessary for one story, frame weather-boarded dwelling 32' × 52', six rooms,

Emma's daughter, Edna, remembers that the barn was built the same year as the Victorian-style house.

The large size of the barn is evident from the inside. This view also captures the beauty of the functional structure.

hall, bathroom, small pantry and one screened and one open porch, one room and pantry ceiled overhead and inside with beaded ceiling and the remainder with #2 grade flooring. Cost: $1187.70.

1918   A. D. Stahl to F. Stein and Son
One story frame dwelling with four rooms, one hall, one pantry, one screened porch, and one open porch. Cost: $1050.

The Beckmanns' one-story Victorian-style house is built of wood, has three rooms, unscreened front and back porches, an attic, a shingle roof, and pressed tin siding. It is located some distance from the builders in Fredericksburg; though not as large as the more expensive houses, it is somewhat larger than the least expensive structures described in the Mechanics Lien Records. If it had been built between 1915 and 1918, I would guess that it cost under one thousand dollars. Edna Beckmann Hightower had told me that the barn was built in the same year as the house. It is a good-sized barn, but perhaps it cost under five hundred dollars, judging from the price of structures in the lien records. She also told me she thought her parents were able to afford both structures in the same year because of cotton prices. Cotton was the Beckmanns' cash crop. *What happened to the cotton market in the second decade of the twentieth century? And how did that affect Emma's life?*

The chart on the opposite page is a composite of market price listings which appeared in the *Fredericksburg Standard* for the dates indicated. Note the changes in the price of the listed commodities.

Finding references to the cotton market was easy. Several books on the topic told more than I wanted to know about the crop, its problems, its limitations and advantages, and its history. Back issues of big-city newspapers for 1914, 1915, 1916, and 1917 carried cotton price quotations prominently placed on their business pages. I went to the Fredericksburg newspaper to find price quotations that would have most directly affected Emil and Emma's crop. Cotton prices were listed with those for other farm products like butter and eggs, corn, and even hens. Like every-

	July 8, 1916	Sept. 23, 1916	Nov. 24, 1916
Butter	15¢/lb.	15¢/lb.	17.5¢/lb.
Eggs	12½¢/doz.	18¢/doz.	30¢/doz.
Corn	50¢/bushel	65¢/bushel	90¢/bushel
Hens	8¢/lb.	10¢/lb.	11¢/lb.
Cotton (at Fredericksburg)	12.25¢/lb.	15.21¢/lb.	20¢/lb.
Cotton Seed	30¢/ton	40¢/ton	50¢/ton

	Feb. 23, 1917	June 2, 1917
Butter	25¢/lb.	25¢/lb.
Eggs	25¢/doz.	25¢/doz.
Corn	95¢/bushel	$1.20/bushel
Hens	13¢/lb.	13¢/lb.
Cotton (at Fredericksburg)	15.5¢/lb.	20¢/lb.
Cotton Seed	40¢/ton	(no quotation)

thing else, the price of cotton increased from 1916 to 1917, the rise being fairly steady. That progression is clear in the sample of price quotations. The *San Antonio Express-News* and the *New York Times* of 1915 to 1918 also show cotton prices rising to over thirty cents per pound in 1918. The reason? World War I.

An interesting article appeared in the Fredericksburg *Standard* of June 24, 1916:

The Cotton Crop of 1915

Washington, D.C., June 22, 1916.—A bulletin on cotton production in the U.S., just issued by Director Sam L. Rogers, of the Bureau of the Census, Department of Commerce and prepared under the supervision of Mr. William M. Steuart, chief statistician in charge of the inquiry, shows the American cotton crop of 1915— 11,191,820, equivalent 500-lb. bales—to have been the smallest since 1908. . . .

The increase in the production of linters during recent years is noteworthy. Starting at 114,544 bales in 1899, the output of this product increased to 880,780 bales in 1915. The 1915 linter product even exceeded that of the cotton crop of 1915 by nearly 24,000 bales, although the cotton crop of 1915 was very much smaller than that of 1914. This increase in linter production is due to some extent to closer delinting of the seed from the better separation of the meat from the hulls, but more especially to the high prices obtained for the fiber, which is used extensively in the manufacture of gun-cotton and smokeless powder. Many mills now obtain considerably more than 100 lbs. of linter per ton of seed treated, whereas in earlier years 50 lbs. per ton was a high yield. . . .

Texas alone produced 3,227,480 bales, or more than one-fourth of the total crop of 1915.

A new wrinkle—another twist—now appeared. Cotton had not been an abundant crop in the nation in 1915. However, Texas was producing a substantial portion of the country's cotton. Even more important, ginning procedures apparently had improved so that the short fibers of cotton that stick to the seed (the "linters," according to the dictionary) could be extracted. Those short fibers might not be good enough for making cotton fabric, but they were quite adequate to use for products the war effort required: guncotton and smokeless powder. So, as cotton farmers, Emma and Emil had several things going for them:

1. The demand for their major cash crop was increasing because of the need for guncotton and powder.
2. Ginning procedures were improving to the point where little cotton was lost.
3. Short cotton fibers, once of low value, were acceptable for the production of ammunition.
4. In 1916, Emil had doubled their land holdings, which could have had a sizeable effect on their cotton crop.

How much cotton might Emil have produced in a year on his farm between 1915 to 1918? Charles Weinheimer told me:

Most cotton farmers in the Albert-Stonewall area planted about fifty or sixty acres of their two-hundred-acre farms in cotton. That's all a man could manage with a single row planter, a single row cultivator, and a team of horses. Cotton was their only cash crop. They'd get about half a bale to an acre. A bale of cotton, after it's ginned, weighs five hundred pounds. But if there was rain or the boll weevils were bad, the crop would be less.

Cotton pickers usually got about fifty cents per hundred pounds. If you could pick two hundred pounds a day, you could earn a dollar. Usually there'd be families to do this work. Some were Mexican families that would live in a cabin on the farmer's land most of the year and chop and pick the cotton when it was time. Other times, they'd work around the farm—the parents and the children. Sometimes, though, families would come in just for the season and they'd camp near the fields. A farmwife could sell eggs and milk to them.

Even with these estimates of the economics of cotton in the area during the time Emma and Emil probably built their house, I couldn't be sure just what they earned from their cotton crop without an intensive study of the economics of growing cotton in the area. Many questions needed answering:

How many acres of the four-hundred-acre farm did Emil plant in cotton?

How many laborers did he need to chop and pick that cotton? What did he pay them?

How much did the ginner charge?

What was the quality of his cotton?

What was the cost of upkeep of his equipment? Did he have blacksmith fees that influenced his profit each year?

Were there boll weevil and water problems affecting his crop?

What price per pound of cotton did Emil actually get?

The best I could do was estimate Emil's earnings based on the price quotations in the newspaper and information from Stonewall residents about cotton farming around World War I. Emil might have produced about thirty bales of cotton from planting sixty acres. The information Charles Weinheimer had given me suggested that Emil would not have been able to cultivate all four-hundred acres unless he had more or better machinery than most, which was unlikely. It seems that he could have produced about 15,000 pounds of cotton in a year. At twelve cents a pound, the market value of that crop would have been $1800. At fifteen cents per pound, the market price at Fredericksburg in September 1916, a thirty-bale yield would have been worth $2250. Since Emma and Emil produced their own food, their major expenses would have been hiring field hands, ginning their harvest, repairing equipment and using the blacksmith's services, and purchasing necessities such as clothing, medicines, and sundry household items. If they were frugal, they would probably have seen a profit of several hundred dollars a year. As the price of cotton rose during the war years, they could have accumulated a substantial amount of cash, enough to pay off notes on land and to build a barn and a new house. That house might well have been the type of dwelling that the nineteen-year-old bride was thinking about when she drew up her wish list on the end papers of a book on agriculture. Perhaps that was prophesy. It may be that Emma would have gotten her own house whether or not the First World War had driven up cotton prices. Several interpretations of the data are plausible: they might have saved their money over many years; they might have borrowed money; they might have been given money that is unrecorded; or maybe they sold something they made or had that increased their ready cash. Exactly what made it possible for Emma and Emil to build their house and barn when they did will probably never be known for sure. But I think that they could not have built so nice a home and a large barn and paid off over $5000 in notes on land without the steady rise in the value of cotton between 1915 and 1918. The effect of World War I on cotton prices places Emma's life—a life lived so conventionally within a twenty-mile radius of the place where she was born—in a larger political context. World events touched Emma's life.

The war affected Emma's life in several ways. Local residents told me that many of the young men in her community were drafted or enlisted in the armed services. Some she knew well from church. Her brother-in-law, Max, one of Emil's younger brothers and a witness at her wedding, entered the service. As one who conversed more often in German than in English, Emma would have keenly noticed the shift from public use of German to more widespread use of English in the Texas Hill Country when America entered the war. No doubt she heard about the war when she went to town. Reports of the battles were in the local news-papers; the German language paper, *Das Wochenblatt,* which tena-ciously continued in print through the war years, carried reports of the German threat from the German-American perspective. Whether or not Emma read the papers, she probably heard some of the issues they raised discussed in shops, at church, and even in her own kitchen. She may have voiced her own ideas about them too. That is, of course, pure conjecture. Emma kept no diary, and no one alive today can remember that far back to what she might have said over the dinner table at home or the picnic table on church grounds. But the war influenced the economics of Emma's life. And that fact underscored another aspect of human experience in any age: one man's misfortune is another man's gain.

Emma's Story

HURSDAY, June 29, 1916
Emma peered through the back window of the room where she was mending cotton sacks. She had stopped to rest for a minute. The work tired her eyes. Thick canvas was not easy to work with. It broke her needles and it produced nothing of beauty. She could see the hen house and several hens running about the yard. She liked her hens. They repaid her for the work she did to keep the hen house in order with eggs, dozens of eggs she could sell to the day laborers Emil hired. The egg money grew to nice sums sometimes. Thanks to her hens, Emma had never made a trip to town penniless. She turned away from the bright outside light to the more dimly lighted room. The abrupt change blinded her for a moment. She saw large circles of light on the cotton sack she had been mending. Knowing their cause, she closed her eyes and waited. When she opened them again, the cotton sack was once more clearly defined. Emma set herself back at the task of mending it.

Beads of sweat formed on Emma's brow as she bent over the tough sewing job. This summer of 1916 was as hot and humid as usual. She was uncomfortable, but the work had to be done. The cotton crop was ready to pick.

Twenty-one-month-old Elgin stirred in the crib nearby. Emma felt the boy's perspired skin and removed the sheet that covered him. She stroked his yellow-blond hair—such a contrast to her own coloring. Edna, almost six now, had fallen asleep with her doll on the floor of the porch. Emma could see the child through the doorway. The sultry afternoon encouraged napping. She wished that she could indulge herself in some sleep. She blinked away the sandy feeling in her eyes and set the treadle of her sewing machine in motion again.

The task of mending cotton sacks required little thought. Emma worked steadily and with the skill developed by many hours of practice. To resist the temptation of sleep, she allowed a recurring dream to play out in her thoughts.

In her mind's eye, Emma saw a house—one she had waited eight years so far to have. It looked like the one she had grown up in: three large rooms all connected to a hallway that led from front to back porches. Doors would lead into the house at four locations—two at the front, one at the back and one at the side. Windows would allow plenty of light into every room. They would be dressed with lacy curtains like those her mother hung on the windows Emma had looked out of as a child. The front porch would have a swing. And there would be gingerbread trim, lots of it, on front and back porch canopies. It would be so lovely, she thought, so much nicer than the house she was now living in with Emil and their three children. She began to imagine how she would furnish each room. She was just picturing where she would place the Victorian couch and the vase of peacock feathers when she heard the rhythmic crunch of Reuben's bounding gait on the gravel and dirt of the front yard. The boy was heavy-footed even for an eight-year-old. He had been in the fields with his father. His arrival reminded Emma that suppertime was near.

Emma met her son at the doorway to the kitchen. Emil soon followed, looking pensive. She greeted him, making no comment about his thoughtful demeanor.

Meals with the children were always a bit hectic. The heat of summertime seemed to impregnate the house, making the children cranky. She didn't question Emil about his thoughts at the table. Instead, she talked about the smoked sausage they were eating being among the last of the meats from the smokehouse. It alarmed her, she told him, to walk into the smokehouse and see meatless racks.

"When will the butcher club be meeting?" she asked.

"Monday, at the Weinheimer place," Emil told her. "We can be one of the first. There's a couple of calves out there that'd do. Better get the meat sacks out."

Emma was relieved to hear that the butcher club would be meeting the following week. That meant that she would be getting some fresh meat soon enough and for the rest of the summer. She had just enough smoked meat to get them through another week. Fortunately, the garden was doing well, producing a steady supply of green vegetables for the table. Her corn was plentiful this summer too. And she had already begun fermenting several crocks of a bountiful cabbage crop to replenish the family's supply of sauerkraut.

That was the sum of dinner conversation, with some chatter from the children. After eating, Emil went back outside to do a few more chores before the light was gone. Emma cleared the table and set some water on the stove to heat for washing.

Dishwashing seemed never-ending. By evening, Emma had seen enough of dirty dishes and greasy dishwater in the dishpans on the kitchen table. Carrying bucketsful of water from the supply that the windmill pumped out from under the thick limestone terrain was tiring work, especially at the end of days made longer by the summer solstice. But it had to be done. She poured some heated water into the dishpan, saving enough for later use by the children, Emil, and herself. She watched as the hot water and lye soap worked together to cut the grease on the dishes. Scrubbing with a dish cloth aided that action. Dousing the dishes in rinse water finished it. When she dried them with towels she had made from flour sacks, they were spotless.

Emma bathed little Elgin, then called Edna and Reuben in to go to bed. The children were obedient. They responded immediately and began the well-established routine of undressing to their underwear and washing face and hands. Both enjoyed this time in the evening with their mother, especially while she washed and dried their feet, dirtied by their barefoot wanderings in the yard. Emma would tell them stories during this quiet time, help them recite their evening prayers, and tuck them into bed. It was a time of human warmth and personal care that the children secretly looked forward to; sometimes they struggled to stay awake to prolong this quiet, loving time with their mother who never left until sleep overtook them.

Emil returned to the kitchen. The last of the day's sunlight was spent. The flame of a lighted coal oil lamp flickered shadows across the roughly planed wood of the homemade table. Another lamp's tin reflector fanned light into the room. Emma put a steaming cup of brown coffee at Emil's place and poured one for herself. She sat down opposite him. This was their time to talk. Tonight, cotton was on their minds.

"Looks like we'll have a good crop," he told her, then continued, mostly thinking out loud: "The weevils didn't get so much this year. Good thing we bought out Otto when we did. The extra acreage gives us a lot more cotton. Helps make up for weevil damage."

"How many workers will you hire?" Emma needed to know how many sacks to make.

"Think a family of five or six will do to work the fields."

"They'll be staying for several months to chop and pick, won't they?" Emma was wondering how many dozen eggs she might be able to sell to the workers. Maybe she could sell them some butter too. That would nicely augment her supply of cash.

Emil nodded. "Three or four months should do it."

"Do you think we'll be able to think about a new house soon?" Emma's dream of a fine house was growing more intense. "Now that Otto's gone, we can make the kitchen where he lived." Wanting to make a strong case for the house, she added, "This one's too small for three children."

"The price of cotton's been going up," Emil responded.

"Opa says"—Emma referred to her father as she had taught the children to—"that the war in Europe is doing that."

"Guncotton." That's all Emil said. He tended to speak sparingly and mostly in phrases. Emma knew how to fill in the gaps.

"What will that do for us?" Emma was still thinking about her house.

"It's over twelve cents a pound these days. Some say won't be long before it's fifteen or more. Maybe will be by the time we're ginning ours."

He was right. By fall of that year, cotton was selling at fifteen cents per pound. In August, Emma had watched the cotton pickers move down the rows of stalks topped with fluffy white bolls. With Emil, she had anxiously watched ominous clouds with dark bellies move over those fields. With Emil, she breathed more easily when clear skies came back into view and the ground stayed dry.

Some of the pickers had a talent for the task. The long sacks trailed behind them like trains from the strap they slung over their shoulders. As they moved along the rows of cotton plants, the sack, looking at first like a shriveled string bean, swelled until it seemed ready to burst. And when it was hooked on the scales, they seemed almost to echo the grunt of the man who hoisted the sack, using the wire loop at its corner to double it on itself, so no part rested on the ground during weighing. Emma had enough experience with cotton to know how to look for evidence of too much cotton boll in with the cotton. The best workers filled their sacks with next to none. Pure cotton meant more profit.

Emma watched Emil take the last wagonload of cotton to Eckert's gin. Many hours later, he returned. He walked into the room where he kept the family ledger locked away from the children's curious hands. He made a notation, then studied the page. Emil turned and carried the carefully kept financial record into the kitchen where Emma was baking bread.

"Next year," he said. Emma noted the rare twinkle that came to Emil's eye when he was feeling prosperous. She knew that he was talking about the new house.

By December of the year, Emma and Emil had saved enough to pay almost two thousand dollars toward the debt they had incurred to buy Otto's land. In the same month as Emma's twenty-ninth birthday, they paid the last installment on the note to Emil's father for some of the land they had acquired as newlyweds. It had taken ten years to get that deed. Now they owned over two hundred acres outright.

On April 2, 1917, President Woodrow Wilson called the nation to arms. The United States was entering the "war to end all wars," the president told the nation. Emma had not thought much about the world war—the European war—that was being fought so far from her home. She didn't know much about wars. She didn't know much about politics. She hadn't read much since she stopped going to school. There were few books in the house besides Reuben's school texts—Emma didn't even use a cookbook. The family subscribed to no magazines. Once in a while, Emil would get a copy of *Das Wochenblatt,* and sometimes a back issue of the *Fredericksburg Standard* found its way into Emma's world. But most of the news she heard was gotten by word of mouth from her sister or Maria Behrens, her closest neighbor and friend, or members of Trinity Lutheran Church who gathered for worship and conversation on Sundays. The president's announcement brought the war closer to home. Every time she turned around, it seemed to Emma that people were talking about "the war." And those instances increased as the names of young men from the community were published in the *Standard*—those called to arms. There was something else too: a defensiveness about being German-American that surfaced in varied ways, especially the public use of English rather than German.

For Emma and Emil, the war meant prosperity. Cotton prices continued to rise in response to the need for guncotton and smokeless powder. For Emma, in particular, the war made possible the one thing she had longed for since she was a bride of nineteen: a house like the one she grew up in, a house that she could decorate and furnish nicely, a house in which she could entertain people in style: a house with a porch and parlor.

Wednesday, May 9, 1917

Emma dressed carefully on a slightly muggy day. Her body had thickened considerably since the birth of her children. She was glad that corsets were no longer required to be well-dressed in town. She put on a simple suit of brown broadcloth. Its slim ankle-length skirt hung from the waistband without decoration or drape. She had recently let out the seams to make it fit better. She tucked a white batiste blouse into the waistband and put on a single-breasted boxy jacket. Instead of the bonnet that usually covered the dark brown hair she still wore in a style of her girlhood, Emma placed a deeply-cuffed brown straw on her head. She studied herself for a moment in the dresser mirror. It was especially important to look right today. She was going to Fredericksburg to pick out the gingerbread pattern for her new house.

Emil called to her, and she called to the children. Emma placed a long white scarf over her hat, tying it under her chin. This done, she nodded to Emil and the five-member family headed for Fredericksburg in their wagon.

When they got to town they headed directly for the lumber yard and store of F. Stein and Son, the major builder and building supplier in the area. What they arranged to do today they would live with the rest of their lives. They were not likely to get another house. This one had to be done right.

Little Edna and Elgin needed no reminding. They demonstrated remarkable self-discipline, sitting quietly where their parents told them to sit, waiting for minutes that seemed like hours to pass as their parents transacted business they didn't understand. Reuben stayed with his father. After all, he was almost ten. He needed to learn how to conduct business. Emil was negotiating for one of the most important things in anyone's life in the Texas Hill Country. The boy would learn about lumber, tin siding, hardware, molding, and all the things that go into the construction of a house. He'd also learn how to strike a bargain.

While Emil worked at that, Emma settled down to talk with the clerk who was showing her the gingerbread patterns. They conversed in English. He expressed some regret that this was one of his last days in the store. He was going into the army in a few days. He told Emma that he was looking forward to serving his country. But she could see beyond the bravado. He was scared.

The gingerbread trim for the porches of her new house had to be just right. Emma studied pages of diagrams. There were many patterns to choose from. She narrowed the choice to six before consulting Emil.

"Which do you like?" she asked him.

"The cheapest one," was the expected answer.

Emma was not about to choose by price alone. "Look at these two," she directed, placing side by side the diagrams of trims priced at about the middle of the range of prices represented by the original set of six. One featured a diamond shape, the other was more square.

"Which do you want?" Emil asked, urging his wife to make the choice.

She looked intently at the diagrams, turning them around, placing them next to one another, and studying each minute detail. "This one, I think." Emma pointed to the diamond cutout flanked by teardrops, pointed end to end.

"Are you sure?"

"I'm sure." Emma could see the trim along the edge of the roof of the L-shaped porch. She imagined how it would appear painted a bright white and supported by decoratively curled braces of wood at each corner where trim met smoothly planed posts. "I'm sure," she added.

Emma watched her house take shape in the months that followed. It was an exciting, rich time for her. The house was exactly as she had envisioned it, neither grand nor fancy, but suited to her taste. The price of cotton continued to rise as the war extended into yet another year. Emma chose to decorate the parlor and master bedrooms with lightly striped wallpapers—different patterns for different rooms but all light in color. Emma liked light coming through windows and doors and reflected by walls. It made the rooms look bigger, she thought. She bought area linoleum of good quality to cover the floors that would get most of the traffic, the floors in what would become the children's room and the master bedroom. The kitchen in the stone building got linoleum too. Emma knew that the kitchen floor would have to be tough, so she bought the best they could afford for it. She supervised its installation and the installation of the piece of equipment she would use without fail every day of her life: the new range.

Emil drove the wagon to Fredericksburg to pick up the new range that had arrived by train all the way from St. Louis via San Antonio. Emma went about her work all morning of that spring day and through the afternoon, feeling impatient by four o'clock when there was still no sign of Emil. She hadn't gone with him because it was much easier to tend the children at home and there really wasn't much she could do to help with the freight. She wished that she could have, though. She had been waiting for it for so long that she felt she couldn't wait another minute.

Emil didn't arrive until dusk. He had taken the opportunity

to visit with friends and shop for hardware in town. Emma had to wait until the next day to see what was packed in the large crate that seemed to fill the wagon.

Early, very early the next morning, Emma insisted that Emil unpack the crate and install her new range before the builders got started again on the house that was going up on the other side of the *durchgang*. As the men wrenched, the sides of the wooden crate dropped away to reveal a complete four-burner nickel-plated blue steel range. It had all the marvelous features Emma had made do without for so many years: a large oven with a door that dropped down easily and remained level while open, a removable porcelain-lined reservoir where she could keep water hot, a wood-feed door and a large pan to collect the ashes, a warming closet above the cooking surface where she could keep warm the foods that were cooked first as she prepared dinner, even a recessed flue running up its back. What marvelous meals she could prepare now, she thought as she watched the men push, pull, and carry the large stove into the kitchen. They angled it against the wall with the window looking out into the back yard and attached the stove pipe to the range's flue back and out the flue opening at the top of the wall. When everything was in place, Emma watched with the children and the men who had helped as Emil stoked the firebox with logs and set the first fire to cook the first meal on the new range in Emma's new kitchen. Everyone caught the party-like mood. They joked and laughed with one another. And, of course, everyone had to touch the stove before it got too hot. Emma ran to the log house to unpack her best apron, the one she had edged with tatting around the bib and at the hem. The first meal she cooked on her new range was going to be cooked in style. It wasn't long before the unmistakable scent of yeast and cinnamon drifted out the kitchen door, over the outside hallway and into the rooms of the house that the workers were finishing with beaded wood, stained wainscoting, and wallpaper. Moist chewy sweet rolls would soon be ready to help fill the growing voids in their bellies.

The room of the house that Emma treated with the most tender care was the one the family would use least often. Into the parlor she moved the sofa and chairs that she had kept covered in the back room of the house she had lived in since her wedding day. She added a new Victorian-style couch, the type she sometimes imagined herself lounging on—if she could ever find some time away from house and farm duties. Into the parlor, she moved her best lamp tables and coal oil lamps, a cabinet with glass doors that she could lock away from the children, and a wool area rug. Emma dressed the windows with lacy curtains like the ones her mother had used.

It wasn't until November of 1918 that she got the peacock feathers. She had expressed a desire for some quite casually at one of the family gatherings on a Sunday after church. Her sister Ella heard and made note. She brought a gift of several nicely colored ones. The two sisters enjoyed choosing the best place to display them in the parlor.

Emma placed the peacock feathers in a treasured crystal vase she had gotten as a wedding present and put it on the table beside the couch. She stepped back to examine the effect. She was standing parallel to the parlor doorway, in full view of the children's room that led to the outside hallway. Reuben bounded onto the wooden floor of that *durchgang*. He spied his mother through the line of open doorways and announced, in a matter of fact way: "The war's over. Teacher said so."

Emma was startled more by the intrusion on her thoughts than the message. Reuben is rambunctious, she reminded herself. She looked around the room. It looked so nice, so genteel, like a proper parlor. Satisfied with the way she had finished this room she had wanted for so many years, she turned her attention back to the intruder. "The war's over," she parroted her son's words.

"I'm hungry, Mama," Reuben called.

Emma's eyes embraced the room once more—they ran down the beige-and-white striped wallpaper, along the molding that edged the dark wainscoting, and across the lacy curtains cascading over its tall windows. The peacock feathers added just the right touch of color.

"The war's over." The importance of that information had not quite sunk in yet. "Time it was," she thought and headed for the kitchen to make her schoolboy a snack.

Finding Life Stories

HERE is no single correct way to research a life story. Too many variables can influence the process and the findings of humanities detective work. Each investigation is as unique as the primary personalities involved: the researcher and the subject. The process is also greatly influenced by the sources of information available at a given time. The types of artifacts and the particular informants that the humanities detective can find will not be the same for every life story or even for the same life story researched at different times. That is what makes this type of inquiry so exciting. The stories of human lives are not reconstructed in a controlled laboratory setting; they weren't lived out in neatly organized ways. They're reconstructed through a fascinating mixture of intuitive and rational thinking. The humanities detective must be a creative questioner, a persistent seeker of clues, a discriminating judge of evidence, and a pattern finder who can look at the "facts" from several perspectives and, from the diverse pieces, reconstruct unrecorded life experiences. The humanities detective must entertain an often complex, even ambiguous kaleidoscope of ideas about the life under study in order to uncover a precious few characteristics of that life. Humanities detective work has its emotional highs and lows. Sometimes, you have to cope with frustrating dead ends. But those times pale by comparison with the exhilaration of each find. Just like the process of the detective work itself, a process that no one can really tell you exactly how to conduct, no one can adequately depict the feelings engendered by the search. All anyone can do is suggest and encourage. That's the purpose of this chapter. The sections that follow offer some guidelines and suggestions for:

Selecting Your Historic Persona
Finding a Collaborator
Using Signpost Artifacts
Seeking and Finding Items of Evidence
Organizing the Data
Interpreting the Evidence
Telling the Story
Asking the Detecting Questions

Selecting Your Historic Persona

I chose to study Emma Mayer Beckmann because of her house. When I walked through the Victorian-style house that she and Emil had built, I could feel Emma's presence. I wanted to find out who she was, what she did, what she experienced, and even what she thought about. Some of my curiosity about Emma was fueled by my unfamiliarity with rural life. The everyday living commonplace to people in Emma's community was a world apart from my big-city upbringing. That difference gave my search for Emma's story a depth of interest that was sustained far longer than might have been possible if our backgrounds had been similar. If they had been, I might have known too much to make the search for her everyday life story as enlightening as it turned out to be. I might have taken too much for granted. My search for Emma's story was true inquiry because there was so much about the "dailiness" of her life that I didn't know. There was so much about Emma's world that I needed to learn if I was going to understand her. And I wanted to understand her. I wanted to make her come alive in my mind's eye. Emma's house provided a context for her life story. I pretended to see her moving about within it, doing the things she typically did.

The following guidelines are drawn from my experience in choosing Emma as my historic persona; they may help you make a discriminating choice of your own:

1. Start with an artifact that contains some clues to a person's life rather than the name of a candidate for study. If the artifact is representative of the time and place of an individ-

ual life, it can set you on a path of exploration rich in diverse directions for inquiry. Look for an important possession or a collection of personal possessions. An individual's dwelling is an ideal place to begin, but it is not the only artifact that can prompt exciting humanities detective work. Several seemingly less significant artifacts taken together can give clues to what the person may have done or experienced in one or more periods of his life. The best search emerges from a solid starting place. So find the artifacts first; then look for the person behind them.

2. Every life is worthy of study. Whether or not you choose to study one or another depends primarily on two factors: (1) whether you have or can find sufficient information about that life to make the inquiry successful and (2) how much interest you have in the person. The individual whose artifacts you have access to should be inherently interesting to you for whatever reason: gender, era, occupation, achievements, problems, influence, lifestyle, or even relationships to yourself or others you know. You must have a keen interest to sustain you through the frustrating times when information seems scarce and the clues you need are hard to find.

3. Pick someone whose life was sufficiently different from your own to make the search challenging. Humanities detective work is not much fun if it produces little learning. While no two people have exactly the same life experiences, if you and your persona have similar backgrounds, you may not think to question some things and, for lack of a question, important differences may be lost. We tend to take the mundane for granted. So, for instance, because I know that impatiens are planted in pots, I didn't ask what kind of pots Emma used for her flowers. I assumed that those pots would be clay, like the ones that contain my impatiens. But Emma didn't have clay pots. She probably would have used iron pots. I hadn't thought to ask about something that seemed to be common knowledge. "Common" knowledge often changes from time to time. I learned to ask about everything.

4. Many questions about the person whose life you choose

to study should fill your thoughts from the very beginning of your detective work. If the questions are numerous at the start, the likelihood is that they will continue to flow as you gain more information. If they are few and far between in the beginning, that may be a signal that your sense of direction for the inquiry is unclear. It could mean that your interest in your persona is insufficient to promote the study. If a paucity of questions suggests that your study lacks direction or interest, reevaluate your choice. Without a clear focus and strong enthusiasm for the inquiry, you'll be put off by the dead ends that lie just around the bend of every search for any life story. Let your questions be your guide and choose your subject as carefully as you would a friend.

Finding a Collaborator

I first met Ophelia Nielsen Weinheimer at the state park where Emma's house is part of a living history reconstruction. Ophelia works there as an interpreter of farm life in Emma's era. She was born and reared on a farm in the same community Emma knew. Like Emma, Ophelia reared her own family there. She is also a teacher. All of these things, combined with her keen interest in local history, caused Ophelia to be enthusiastic about my interest in researching Emma's story. Her experience and capabilities made it possible for her to play Dr. Watson to my Sherlock Holmes. If it hadn't been for Ophelia, I would not have been able to locate and talk to people who gave me information about Emma's time and place. On many occasions, she gained access for me to people who know and respect her; they agreed to talk to me because they trust her. Ophelia offered me direction and support, helping me solve problems and reacting to my ideas. She kept me accurate and honest as I interpreted the data I had collected. She helped me decide when to let go of a question or line of inquiry for which there were no ready answers and when to persevere. I couldn't have detected as much of Emma's story as appears in this book without her collaboration.

We all need allies and critics to help us sort out the wheat from the chaff in our humanities detective work. Without them, the search can be lonesome. But even more important, with a collaborator who is also a respected member of the community, you may have access to sources of information that you couldn't gain by yourself. Further, it's satisfying to share the excitement of your finds with a partner and comforting to have support during the frustrating times.

Once you have selected your historic persona, talk about your plans for detecting that person's life story and note the people whose eyes light up at the thought and who volunteer ideas for the study. From those who seem genuinely interested in your project, at least one will emerge as a potential collaborator. You may want to put together a team of detectives, but I recommend finding one partner who is a respected member of the community in which your persona lived, who likes people, and who might be described as patient, thoughtful, and questioning. Then start talking about the life you wish to reconstruct. Together, ask questions and look for the artifacts that supply clues to their answers. Together, interpret and reinterpret your findings; challenge one another's assumptions. Then imagine your persona alive in his or her own time in scenarios you play out for one another. That sharing will help you discover what you don't know and what you can find out.

Using Signpost Artifacts

Every life has its own chronology, but the sequence of events from birth to death, with the common events along the way, is not always evident during humanities detective work. Although life stories needn't be told in a particular sequence, a timeline helps the researcher gain a sense of which events were contingent upon others in a person's life, which influenced others, and which seemed independent of one another. In my search for Emma's story, I became more aware of the significance of dates than I had ever thought possible, given my somewhat disdainful attitude toward the prevalence of dates in history textbooks. I realized that I had to have them and recall them in order to understand contexts and connections in Emma's life. Clues to her life experiences didn't come to me in clearly organized or sequenced ways. They came in odds and ends, in bits and pieces, in jumbled arrays. Some were clearly more important than others in suggesting new directions for study; some were representative of different eras in Emma's life. I found it necessary to sort these out from the rest. They became my "Signpost Artifacts," so-called because they spoke to me of different times along the continuum of Emma's life and because they suggested questions for further study. My signpost artifacts for the part of Emma's life that I chose to reconstruct were her wedding portrait, her wish list, a Watkins Company bottle, and the Victorian-style house. Each in its own way intrigued me. Each in its own way prompted lots of questions. All four, taken together, helped to narrow the primary focus of my search for the years from 1907 to 1918. They anchored my inquiry so that, while I could move as far afield from those artifacts in Emma's life as I chose, I couldn't make too many detours without being reminded of my original purpose. Accordingly, my search for Emma's story led me back to the time of her birth in 1888, her childhood, and her young adulthood, but not past her years as young wife and mother through to her old age. The signpost artifacts directed me to so many items of evidence pertaining to the first three decades of Emma's life that I felt no compelling desire to explore her later years. The decision to focus on Emma's early life was based on personal interests spawned by the artifacts I discovered and the challenging questions they raised in my mind. Each humanities detective will make different choices and ask different questions. That's what makes the process creative.

Despite this emphasis on Emma's early life experiences, information about her later years cropped up from time to time. Of the Beckmanns' three children, only Edna lived with them all their lives. Both sons married and started families in their youth. Edna married late in life and had no children of her own. Emil died in 1951. Emma lived for another ten years, with Edna and her husband, in the Victorian-style house. At Emma's death, Edna inherited the farm, and Emma's will cites the daughter's loyalty and devotion. Shortly after Emma's death the farm was bought by the Texas State Department of Parks and Wildlife to create the Living History Farmstead. The lavatory, running water and electricity added by Emma and Emil in their later years were removed, and the house was restored to its 1915–1918 condition, as it was when Emma was a young matron with three small children.

Seeking and Finding Items of Evidence

My signpost artifacts helped focus my thinking so that I had some ideas about what to look for rather than using a shotgun-like approach that seeks anything and everything, wherever and whenever it might be available. Emma's wedding portrait raised questions about when and where and how she was married, how old she was at the time, where the portrait was made, how stylish her wedding clothes were, and what her wedding day might have been like, but along the way of searching for answers to specific questions, I came across traces that proved to be important items of evidence later on in my search. I had not yet thought of the questions each answered; they lacked interest for me until I gained more knowledge of my subject. I found it helpful to photograph and note the location of any artifact I came across that seemed even remotely relevant to Emma's story. Similarly, the notes I made on information offered by people consulted about Emma's story, even if it seemed tangential to my immediate interests, usually proved valuable later in my search. It's easier to re-trace steps that have been recorded than to recover those vaguely recalled. That seems self-evident, but it's easy to forget when you're attempting to make sense out of an avalanche of information or coping with roadblocks and dead ends in an effort to answer one simple question.

Several types of evidence helped in my search for Emma's story:

Personal papers. These can be wonderfully rich sources of information because they are specific to an individual's life. Unfortunately, personal papers are among the first to be discarded unless they are official documents or just happen to have been stored in something that's kept in a drawer or on a shelf—like a book. The only personal paper that I found for Emma was the wish list for her dowry—the one she wrote on the end papers of a book on agriculture. That was a valuable find, but that's all there was. Emma kept no diary. If she wrote letters, they have not survived—at least not in the community in which she lived her entire life. This is more often than not the case for ordinary people, especially those whose lifestyles required physical labor most of the day. Emma could read and write. She simply didn't have the time or inclination perhaps to make written records of her thoughts. I had to be satisfied with the one personal paper of Emma's that I had found, and I became grateful for it.

Personal possessions. Like personal papers, personal possessions are discarded or given away often before their owner's life is over. At first, I wanted to pursue the study of Emma as a purist might, seeking only those items of evidence that were bona fide traces of Emma. I soon discovered that my search would die prematurely if I insisted on maintaining so narrow a criterion for admissible evidence. Just as most of my own personal items are examples of standard merchandise in today's stores and are similar to those used by my contemporaries, so the surviving personal items that belonged to people of Emma's generation and community held clues to those that had been Emma's. The wedding dress that Mrs. Nielsen wore, the tatting that Mrs. Neffendorf did, the school books that children used, the clothing that was advertised in mail order catalogs of the early twentieth century, and the homemade and manufactured turn-of-the-century furniture I saw in various places in Emma's community—all these things could very well have belonged to Emma. She was more like than unlike others of her place and time. She lived as her neighbors lived, so the artifacts of her era in her community are also artifacts of Emma's life—by implication. While keeping in mind that they were not hers, I sought examples of clothing, books, toys, furniture, tools, and sundry household items, whether for work or entertainment or decoration, that could give me some idea of the things of Emma's world. The important criteria for considering other people's artifacts as evidence for Emma's story were whether:

1. The item was used during the period of Emma's lifetime that I was studying.
2. The item was representative of others that were commonplace in the community of that time.
3. Several references verified an item's authenticity for Emma's life and times.

As you seek personal items for your historic persona, you may find that, like personal papers, few exist. Like us, people of earlier times did not choose to save the things they considered useful but banal. So, you may have to search for related items—those that your historic persona could have used, might have owned, and probably made. The members of your subject's community can help with that. What you don't find in one house, you may find in another.

In addition to local residents of Emma's community who could tell me about the lives of their parents and grandparents and who eagerly shared with me their family artifacts, I sought the advice of several historical reference librarians. They were helpful in directing me to articles and books that described the various aspects of historical inquiry. Although those sources on interpreting artifacts, collecting oral histories, examining documents, and finding a wide variety of primary sources treated that inquiry in more formal ways than I could conduct my search into Emma's life, they offered guidelines that made my search easier and truer to the principles of historical research. Such references may not give specific direction to your inquiry into every primary source relevant to your search, but they can help you avoid making serious mistakes.

By establishing contact with at least one historical reference librarian, you can have an objective source of help in assessing the relevance of the personal possessions you uncover. Museum curators are also helpful in this regard. These people can keep you honest, prevent you from being lured by the exotic, and make you attentive to the historical value of mundane things in attics, closets, and dresser drawers.

Photographs. My search for Emma's story was prompted by her house, but it began in earnest with her wedding portrait. That photograph was especially meaningful because it was the first evidence I had of what she looked like. Seeing her as a bride caused me to want to see her at other times in her life: as a child, a teenager, a young mother, a middle-aged matron, and an old lady. I will never forget the thorough delight I felt when, in Emma's nephew's home, a cardboard carton filled with photographs was placed before me. Out of that box came a portrait of Emma, the child, and one of Emma, the teenager. Also in the box were the wedding portrait of Emma's parents, a school picture that included Emma among the youngest members of the group, and even a photograph of her parents and brothers standing in front of the house in which she grew up—the one built in 1899 that still stands on the road to Albert. Those marvelous pictures gave a physical identity to the principal characters in the life story I was researching. I no longer had to imagine what they had looked like at the time I wanted to know them. And there was more: whether the pictures were made in a photographer's studio or in the field, their backgrounds and the poses and clothing of the subjects held clues to attitudes, styles, conditions, and environments of the time. I spent many hours poring over those photographs with a magnifying glass, inspecting even the tiniest of details.

People save photos. They place snapshots in albums as readily as they frame studio portraits for display on walls and living room tables. If you are studying a person from the late nineteenth and early twentieth centuries, it is quite likely that photographs of your subject were made by a photographer in a studio or in the field. Some photos are just waiting to be found in family albums and cardboard boxes. Others can be had for a dollar or two in flea markets or antique shops (like the one where I found a copy of Emma's wedding portrait). Still others are in library collections preserved to document the looks of people, their activities, events, buildings, and even parts of towns. And there are pictures in back issues of local newspapers. All are good sources of visual information about your persona's time and place and experiences—as well as self. They can be examined individually or placed in a chronological sequence. It's informative to compare the photographs of different people made for the same reasons, like wedding portraits, in the same era or across eras. Old photographs can even be used to jog old memories.

People's recollections. Many of my questions about Emma's way of life were answered by people who lived when Emma did. Younger members of the community were helpful too, but their information was second-hand. They remembered what their parents had told them and, while that information was usually quite accurate and relevant to Emma's story, it couldn't hold, for me at least, the authenticity of remembered firsthand experience. Those close to or over ninety years of age were my best informants.

Early in my search, I discovered that old memories do need jogging. It's not enough to ask in general terms about a person's childhood or schooling or courtship. "What do you want to know?" they'd ask. I had to do my homework before I talked to Emma's peers. I had to go to them with specific questions. They were not reluctant to give information. They simply believed that the ordinary events of daily life were of little inherent interest. They wanted to recall the extraordinary events, mostly for my amusement. So I had to ask seemingly inane questions like: "How did you get the water from the well to the kitchen?" and "What did you do in school while you were waiting your turn at recitation?" I didn't know the answers to those questions. My informants thought that everybody did; therefore, those things were not worth mentioning—unless requested.

For my purposes, conducting an oral history interview was too formal and took too much time. The people I interviewed preferred a conversational style, a style more appropriate to "visiting." Often, the person I was visiting would serve me food, and conversation would continue over the table. Paper and pencil were my best ally for maintaining records of those conversations. The notes I made while conversing were cryptic, but as soon as I got home, I transcribed them. Then, to be sure that those notes were accurate, I sent the informant copies of the transcription with a self-addressed, stamped envelope and a request to review what I had written, make corrections and even additions as necessary, and return the notes to me. This proved to be a good way both to verify my understanding of what they had said and my recollection of how they had said it. It also sparked recollections that had not come to mind during our conversation. Several sets of notes were returned to me with significant additions.

I always visited people in their homes after calling them by phone. Sometimes, if the person's health was poor, I asked a family member to select the time of my visit and to explain my purpose in talking with them. One of the people I interviewed was living in a nursing home. She viewed my visit as a special treat. Some of the other women in the visitors' room overheard my questions and volunteered their recollections to verify or underscore what I was being told. (They all raved about Watkins vanilla extract.) I was charmed.

When I could combine artifacts with my questions, the responses of the older people often became more animated and more detailed. Photographs were particularly valuable in this way. The old photo brought them back in time to a place and an occasion. That visual stimulus seemed to resurrect old associations and inspire lots of information about the people in the picture, as well as the event.

Above all, I had to be sensitive to several needs of Emma's peers. The most obvious are: (1) making sure not to overtax them, terminating the interview before they became tired; (2) allowing people to talk about some of their favorite experiences even if unrelated to my inquiry; (3) letting go of a question that the respondent cannot answer, no matter how much I needed an answer; and (4) honoring their wishes to keep some information confidential or to avoid talking about some experiences. Sometimes, what may appear to be an innocuous question can trigger painful memories.

My informants were pleased to share their information with me. My verbal thanks, at the end of the interview, sufficiently expressed my gratitude. But I felt that more was needed. I began to send thank you notes, only to discover to my chagrin that, for a few people, those notes required special trips to the post office on the call of the local postal clerk. At least one person was startled by that. Far more effective and better appreciated was a small gift I could send or bring to the person, something I had learned that he or she liked. For one person, that was a copy of an old photo; for another, it was a pot of impatiens. Those gifts were not necessary, but they expressed thanks to people who were sharing their lives with me in an especially meaningful way.

In summary, I recommend the following guidelines when looking for testimonies about the time and individual you are studying:

1. Develop a set of specific questions about the person, place, or events you are researching.
2. Ask around the community for the names of people who are most likely to be able to answer your questions.
3. Call the person you wish to interview or a member of the family and arrange for a date and time of day that is most convenient and doesn't interfere with established routines.
4. Talk with the person in a conversational style; visit

with your informant rather than conducting a formal interview.

5. Ask for clarification but don't push for more information than the person is willing or able to give.

6. Use artifacts, especially old photographs, to focus your inquiry and to jog memories.

7. Make notes that you can transcribe later; although audio recorders are usually used to collect oral histories, many older people, in particular, may find the machine intimidating.

8. Be sensitive to fatigue or distress in your informant and respond accordingly: terminate the interview, take a break, or change the subject.

9. Ask your informants to review and edit the notes you made of their comments, making sure that you provide some way for them to return the notes to you. (The mail worked well for me. Response time was usually under a week.) If this method is not appropriate, read your notes to your informant over the phone or in a follow-up visit so that needed corrections can be made.

10. Acknowledge your informant's contributions to your research in a way that clearly says "Thanks."

Formal documents. Several organizations and institutions in the community where Emma lived were sources of valuable information. The Gillespie County Clerk's office in the county courthouse contains deed records that tell the story of Emil Beckmann's land acquisitions over time. If necessary, I could have traced all references in those records to the land transactions of Ferdinand Mayer, Emma's father, and Hermann Beckmann, Emil's father. In addition, mechanic's lien records provide information about contracts people drew up with local builders and craftsmen. Even though Emil Beckmann's name is not recorded in those contracts, the arrangements made by other people of his generation suggest prices and possibilities of, for instance, houses like the one Emil and Emma built. The county clerk's office also maintains records of names, ages and births, deaths and wills—all of which I consulted in my search for Emma's story. Each document provides information about the principal subjects (e.g., the parents as well as the child are named in birth records) and also information about others who were involved (e.g., identifying the doctor in attendance and the person making the report), and dates and locations (e.g., when and where the child was born). In the same office, I found records of the establishment of schools in the area and maps of the original land surveys named in school land grants as well as in the deed records of private land holdings.

Down the hall from the county clerk's office in the Gillespie County Courthouse is the office of the county judge. There I found old minutes of school board meetings and school attendance records. Because the county judge's office had also once been the office of the superintendent of schools, the records on file there contain information about such things as school finances and teacher certification. In those records I found reference to the certification of Emma's school teacher, many years after Emma had completed her education.

Downstairs in the courthouse, I found tax records in the Office of the County Tax Assessor/Collector. The assessed valuation of the Beckmann property and the increase in Emil's acreage is recorded over the years in those large bulky ledgers; the graceful pen-and-ink penmanship of early-twentieth-century recorders is informative in its own right.

Emma was reared in the Evangelical Lutheran church. The records of her activities in the church are important indicators of her religious and social experiences. Church pastors were helpful in making old church ledgers available for my perusal. I found Emma's baptism recorded in one church and her marriage in another. I found records of her confirmation and the baptisms and confirmations of her children. I also found records of death for Emma, Emil, and their sons. Each entry also offered additional information, such as names of witnesses where appropriate, family relationships, dates, complete names, and the presiding clergyman. Most of these records contained more information than I could use. Many held clues to other people's life stories. In one ledger I found a pastor's journal; in another, references to special church activities.

One public document rich in clues to Emma's life experiences was the United States Census. In the census for 1900, I found information about land ownership, educational experience, language proficiency, and birthplaces of each member of the Mayer and Beckmann families. Names and ages of each helped me place the family members in relation to one another and in the context of Emma's life story. For instance, the census suggested the interrelationships of the people listed as witnesses to Emma and Emil's wedding in church records. The census was especially useful in helping me reconstruct the family backgrounds of my principal subjects. And it was readily available in microfilm at my local library. My recommendation to any and all humanities detectives is to make a point of examining the census reports for the time of greatest interest to your inquiry. Those reports cannot help but provide interesting information and, perhaps, expose some new clues to the life story of your search.

Other formal documents were not available for my inquiry because of the era and the place in which Emma lived. Some towns might have city directories that are especially useful in locating residences and businesses of a particular year. There was none for Stonewall in the early nineteen hundreds. If Emma had belonged to a social organization, although those records might not be public, I would have asked for access to them to see if she was named for membership and for activity. Business ledgers are informative about customers, transactions, and the prices of items sold. The records of insurance companies can tell about the type and value of a house, its functions, and even the personal possessions of the owners. My experience in searching for Emma's story taught me to explore every available source of information, even if I thought that I already had the answer to my question; sometimes records are contradictory. A skeptical attitude about any piece of information, no matter how solid it seems at first, helps to encourage its verification. The guiding principles are: formulate focused questions; ask for specific answers; consult more than one source.

Maps. One very focused question led me to find the most elusive pieces of information about Emma's world that I needed to track down. The question was: What did the town of Fredericksburg look like in 1908? I searched for an early map of the town in all the logical places: the county courthouse, the local library, the local newspaper, a major university library and several reference libraries, as well as the private papers of senior members of the community. When I complained about not being able to find a map of Fredericksburg in 1908, in a casual conversation with a researcher in the Texas Department of Parks and Wildlife, I got a clue: the fire insurance maps of the Sanborn Insurance Company. There was a set, he told me, in the holdings of a state university library. And later, I discovered that those maps are available on microfilm from the United States Archives. Those maps were like a special gift. Although they didn't depict Fredericksburg of 1908, they did show me what the town looked like in 1902 and in 1910 and, from that, I could infer its characteristics in the year of my primary interest.

Maps are especially valuable documents because they provide an image of the place in which a person lived at a particular time. They offer an accurate basis for viewing an environment through the historic persona's eyes. Although they are not always easy to find, they are well worth the effort required either to locate one or to reconstruct one from clues that skillful questioning can obtain from people, pictures, and other documents.

Newspapers. These are perhaps the most entertaining source of information about a person's environment. I was able to gather a wide variety of information about Emma's environment by reading back issues of the local newspapers of her time. Most of the time, I consulted the papers for answers to specific questions. For instance, when I wanted to know the price of cotton in the period of World War I, I scanned back issues of the *Fredericksburg Standard* for their market price quotations. I also scanned many issues to find advertisements that showed the costs and styles of household and personal items Emma might have used. But equally valuable were the understandings I developed about human issues, attitudes, points of view, priorities, and appreciations by simply reading a Fredericksburg newspaper of 1915 as I do those delivered to my door—from front to back, looking at headlines, stopping to read an interesting article, perusing ads, taking note of announcements and happenings, reading cartoons, studying pictures, and arguing with editorials. I found it interesting, too, just as I do in my own day, to compare the headlines and news stories that appeared in same day issues of the *Fredericksburg Standard, Das Wochenblatt,* the *San Antonio Express,* and the *New York Times.* It was, after all, the newspaper that helped me see Emma's life in a broader political and social context than that of her farming community.

Architecture. Just by walking through Emma's house, I was able to gain a sense of the way in which she lived during those years that most interested me. The house also gave me clues to her aesthetic taste and the Beckmanns' economic situation and values. To be sure, it may not always be possible to find the house in which your historic persona actually lived. But historic structures in the community suggest the types of dwellings that were available. Fredericksburg was the place that Emma thought of as town and, fortunately for my detective work, it has a conservation-minded citizenry. The preserved or reconstructed architecture of the town offered visual information about building materials, architectural styles, home layouts, decorative trims, and a myriad of housing features that, when shared by many homes in an area, speak clearly of lifestyles. Similarities in shops and public buildings as well as the way in which the town itself is laid out are indicators of the community's culture and economic conditions. We preserve the homes of great men and women in order to sense their living patterns through their dwellings. It's possible to read old buildings like those in which the less illustrious lived or shopped or visited to reconstruct the lives of ordinary human beings who preserved and developed their community by doing the mundane things pretty much the way everyone did. Those findings of humanities detective work can help the inquirer transcend individual life stories to describe the common. That too is history.

Organizing the Data

I was never so sure of my memory that I did not make notes or pictures of what I found as my study of Emma's life progressed. Soon I had an abundance of material in the form of notes, books, artifacts, xerox copies, and photographs that needed a clearer organization than my hastily constructed folders labeled with dates, names, places, and activities permitted. At this point in my detective work, I had to decide on what time in Emma's life I most wanted to reconstruct. I selected the period from childhood until the end of World War I because that was the period I was most interested in and it was a time in Emma's life for which I could find a good amount of reliable information.

I organized all the data I had collected according to "chapters" of Emma's early life. They are the chapters of this book. Although they represent a chronology of Emma's life, the sequence follows from an exploration of what I considered to be significant experiences in that life. Any life can be recorded on a dated continuum, but life stories are collections of milestones or significant experiences. Those are the things we remember, and by which we often are remembered.

Interpreting the Evidence

Interpretation of evidence hinges on two components of the detective's inquiry: questioning skill and attitude.

The really good humanities detective is in love with questions and is skilled in the art of questioning. Reading artifacts means asking questions of them. It also means letting the object suggest new questions, that is, being aware of what you don't know, of what the artifact doesn't tell. The best questions come from knowledge, not ignorance. The more you know, the better you know what you need to find out. Yet there is a dilemma here. The more you know, the less likely you are to admit ignorance. Asking an honest question is an admission of ignorance. And asking questions of people who are less experienced or less educated but more knowledgeable of the particular life experiences you wish to learn about demands that you temper your pride.

As important as swallowing your pride when asking questions is being skeptical about your interpretations of clues. The humanities detective who gets closest to the truth always seeks verification of information, no matter how reliable the source. The evidence must prove, beyond reasonable doubt, that something was this way or that. Unless it does, alternative interpretations must be considered and suggested.

I sometimes resisted admitting, even to myself, that I would not be able to find the answer to a question; instead I would find myself pursuing a frustrating and time-consuming search. You have to let go of a question when you cannot find answers that you trust. That is often harder than being persistent in your search for an answer that you believe can be found. There's a delicate balance to be maintained in choosing to persist or desist. Neither choice should be made too soon.

Sometimes questions have a way of going off on a tangent that is interesting but takes you too far afield of the subject. For instance, there were times when I almost lost sight of Emma completely as I got involved with the development of railroads in her area, or the cultivation of cotton, or the experiences of people a generation removed from her. I had to reestablish my purposes and push the new interest away, for the moment at least.

It seemed that I could go on forever, asking more and more questions, getting more and more specific about each event or activity in Emma's life. Knowing when to quit the search for any part of the story was important. Most of the time, I went further than necessary. But when my questions became increasingly distant from my original query, it was time to stop. The principle I learned to apply was this: if I had obtained sufficient information to formulate and answer a general question that clarified my initial "wonderings" and if I could answer that question sufficiently well to reconstruct a sharply focused moving scenario in my imagination, then I had found what I needed.

One of the best ways to check the apparent validity of your interpretations is to share them with others. Even those with little or no knowledge of the subject can react to the plausibility of your logic. If you are working closely with a collaborator from the community, you have a ready source of feedback. The more people who will give an unbiased reaction to your interpretations, the more likely you'll be to arrive at the "truth."

As I got to know Emma Mayer Beckmann, I found myself developing affection for her. She became very real to me, especially when I picked up clues to her personal life that helped me learn about her personal characteristics, needs, and wishes. Because of my growing fondness for her as a human being, I found myself not wanting to acknowledge her limitations. Coping with our feelings about a person may be the most difficult part of humanities detective work. Everyone has weaknesses as well as strengths. Every life has failures as well as successes. The limitations and the problems are often clearly discernible in the evidence. It's important to be able to accept them when you find them and understand them for what they are—no more and no less. It's easy to romanticize a life story. If you're studying a member of your own family, that may be a real danger. But even if you're studying a stranger, the story you reconstruct will be only as true and correct as your open-mindedness permits.

Telling the Story

Emma came alive for me only when I could imagine her walking, talking, eating, sleeping, working, playing, and even thinking. Your first reaction may be: "But you can imagine anything you wish. How is that history?" My response is that imagination increased the depth of my historical research. As Emma came alive in my mind's eye, I became aware of those gaps in my knowledge—gaps not big enough to prevent me from writing a narrative of her story but enough to stop action in my imagined reconstruction. Sometimes I could successfully stage complete scenarios and sometimes I could not. When I couldn't do so— when there were gaps in my knowledge that prevented me from completing the imagined scene—my curiosity about Emma's life was further piqued. Best of all, realizing those gaps helped me to know which questions to ask.

So simple a thing as imagining Emma washing dishes required a great deal more information than I expected. I had to find out how the water was siphoned from the well, into what kind of container, where the container of water was taken, into what the water was poured, how the water was heated, what types of soap and dishcloth were used, where the rinse water was held, and what procedure was used to dry the washed and rinsed plate, cup, cutlery, or pot. Only when I knew those particulars could I follow Emma in mind's eye as she did her dishes. So, imagining her at work actually caused me to learn more about her daily life than merely knowing that she washed dishes in a kitchen without running water. My imagination strengthened my inquiry.

Visualizing your persona doing the things the evidence suggests will indicate several ways to organize information. Your story line will gradually emerge as your persona develops character in your imagination. You will find yourself thinking about that life as a story, then telling the story to others, and finally writing it as historical vignettes. In the process of story-telling, questions from your listeners will develop the story further. An honest detective will have impeccable evidence to support those developments.

Asking Detecting Questions

The power of humanities detective work to uncover life stories is directly determined by the questioning strategies used. As you look for items of evidence, interpret what you find, and reconstruct life experiences, the questions you ask and the way in which you relate questions to one another will advance or retard your search.

In my experience, one questioning pattern has proven consistently productive: a general query leads to a series of specific questions which provide answers that help to formulate a new holistic question. That new question is better informed than the first generalized query could have been. And it carries within it the seeds of a hypothesis. So, for example, as I stood looking at Emma and Emil Beckmann's wedding portrait in the inside hallway of their Victorian-style house, my first query was a rather nebulous wondering about the couple on their wedding day. That set the parameters for my first sequence of questions—I would explore their wedding. Still looking at the portrait, I could now begin asking for specific information: *What was the date of their wedding? What type of day was it? Where did Emma get her dress? Who performed the marriage ceremony? When and where was the portrait made? What type of reception did they have?* Once I had formulated the first few questions, others followed. And all were specific enough for me to work from. They suggested places to go, things to consult, and people to see for the answers. When I located those places, artifacts, and people, they offered clear responses to my questions. And the evidence uncovered by those questions led to a new general question: What did Emma experience on that last day of the life she had lived in her parents' home? At this point, I had some hypotheses. So, in response to that question, I could play out the story of a young German Texan bride's wedding day on December 10, 1907, in a stone farmhouse on the road to Albert.

The process is like working a jigsaw puzzle. All the pieces are strewn about at first. If the pattern is unknown, the first generalized wondering is about that image. Then the quest for the particulars of the image proceeds in a random, spontaneous way until, bit by bit, piece by piece, the pattern emerges. When that happens, you begin to know what to look for in the pieces that may complete portions of the picture. If you're successful in finding them, you begin to form hypotheses about what the finished picture will look like. Those hypotheses enable your mind's eye to form images that you can superimpose on the unfinished puzzle. Then your search becomes more informed, more precise, and more productive. Keeping this puzzle metaphor in mind, consider these excerpts from the questioning strategy that Emma's wish list provoked:

The general query was: *What does the wish list say about Emma's intentions for furnishing her home?* That established the outline of the puzzle.

—*What furnishings are listed?*

—*At what costs?*

—*How do the items listed at the costs indicated compare with those in mail order catalogs and ads of the times?*

—*What changes are evident in Emma's handwritten list?*

—*What might account for them?*

—*What furnishings did Emma most likely already have?*

—*How did Emma's list compare to dowries of other brides of her era?*

—*What clues might Emma's alterations to the wish list and her quoted prices for each listed item suggest about her priorities as a young bride?*

The answers to those questions led to the holistic question I really wanted to answer: *Why would Emma select the furnishings she included in her wish list, of the obviously different qualities indicated by the prices she quoted, for the log house that she knew she would move into as a bride?* My imagined scenario gradually came into full view with all the detailed puzzle pieces in place: I pictured a young woman with romantic notions about what it meant to be a young farmwife in her own home, and I saw that image against the backdrop of realities in the Texas Hill Country in 1907. My initial general "wonderings" about where Emma got her ideas led me on several new but related searches for the particulars of her home rearing, her schooling, and the influence of her peers, church, and community.

My generalized queries, prompted by the wedding portrait, the wish list, the Watkins bottle with its trial mark, and Emma's frame house, gave way to particular questions which, when answered, gave me hypothetical pictures of the whole. That process powered my imagery. I visualized the meanings of each piece of information I obtained and discovered their interactions. To use another metaphor, a cinematic one, there emerged a moving picture of Emma's life experiences, often sharply focused with considerable depth of field, with close-ups and panoramic views, with dialogue, sound effects, and sometimes background music too. Some frames were in black and white; others were in brilliant color. Through them all, Emma was the star.

Emma is very real to me, even though I did not know her when she was alive. Nonetheless, because I came to know and understand and to appreciate her in my search for her story, Emma lives on in my memory.

Your inquiry into the life of another can give that persona a measure of immortality—in your mind if in no other. Humanities detective be warned: the images you form could haunt you for the rest of your life.

Typesetting by G&S, *Austin*
Printing and binding by Edwards Brothers, *Ann Arbor*
Design by Whitehead & Whitehead, *Austin*